TIDMAN'S MEDIA INTERVIEW TECHNIQUE

Handling the media and getting your point across on TV, radio and within your organization

Peter Tidman MBE
H. Lloyd Slater

McGRAW-HILL BOOK COMPANY

London · New York · St Louis · San Francisco · Auckland
Bogotá · Caracas · Hamburg · Lisbon · Madrid · Mexico
Milan · Montreal · New Delhi · Panama · Paris · San Juan
São Paulo · Singapore · Sydney · Tokyo · Toronto

Published by
McGRAW-HILL Book Company Europe
Shoppenhangers Road, Maidenhead, Berkshire, SL6 2QL England
Telephone 0628 23432
Fax 0628 770224

British Library Cataloguing in Publication Data
Tidman, Peter,
  Tidman's media interview technique.
  I. Title II. Slater, H. Lloyd,
  808.53

ISBN 0 07 707577 3

Library of Congress Cataloging-in-Publication Data
Tidman, Peter (Peter Theodore John),
  Tidman's media interview technique: handling the media and getting your point across on TV, radio, and within your organization
  Peter Tidman, H. Lloyd Slater.
      p.   cm.
  Includes index.
  ISBN 0-07-707577-3
  1. Interviewing in mass media. I Slater, H. Lloyd,
  II. Title,
  P96.I54T53 1992   91-35689
  302.23-dc20   CIP

Copyright © 1992 McGraw-Hill International (UK) Limited. All rights reserved. No part of this publication may be reproduced, stored in a retrieval system, or transmitted, in any form or by any means, electronic, mechanical, photocopying, recording, or otherwise, without the prior permission of McGraw-Hill International (UK) Limited.

1234 CUP 9432

Typeset by BookEns Ltd, Baldock, Herts.,
and printed and bound in Great Britain at the University Press, Cambridge.

Contents

Introduction		vii
1.	On the receiving end	1
2.	Just who do you think you are?	8
3.	Grasping the tools of the trade	14
	The memo	15
	The letter	19
	Employee communications	21
	The presentation	24
	The employee forum	30
	The press release	32
	The next step	35
4.	Getting a fair deal from the ace reporter	36
	The inquisition begins	37
	Telling the truth	39
	Face to face	40
	The unexpected call	44
5.	The voice of reason	46
6.	How you fit into the picture	53
	The background	54
	Television: the protocols and the power	59

7.	Television: playing by the rules	63
	Attracting attention	64
	Retaining attention	69
	Leaving a message	72
	Adding it up	76
8.	Just get to the point!	77
	Getting down to the gist	80
9.	Looking beyond the notebook, the smile and the suntan	88
10.	Bright lights, potted plants, make-up and you	96
	Looking the part	101
	Knowing the score	108
11.	In the den of the video lion	111
	Making the most of your brief encounter	116
12.	Playing host to the TV beast	131
13.	You have a story to tell	138
Index		147

Introduction

'By your communication shall ye be known.'
                                    Anon.

This book is about communication in general and communication through the media in particular. It places particular emphasis on that most effective medium of all, television.

As far as communications in general are concerned, you are probably doing quite all right already. After all, your friends, your family, your subordinates at work, your peers and your bosses all seem to have a pretty good idea of what you are getting at most of the time. There might be the odd misunderstanding now and then, and perhaps you don't *always* succeed in conveying your ideas—however brilliant and original they might seem to you—and having them understood and accepted by the people who count. But on the whole you are, no doubt, pretty successful in putting the gist of a point across.

But are 'quite all right' and 'pretty successful' really the standards of communication you aim to achieve? After all, without your thoughts, your opinions, your values, your strategies, your ideas, what are you? And if the subtleties of your cerebral processes are lost in the process of externalizing them in a form readily understandable by others who can act on those thoughts, what good are they?

There is an ancient philosophical teaser that poses the question about what sound a falling tree might make in a forest with no human being or animal around to hear it. The answer—despite all the energy unleashed in the mighty crash—is a poignant silence. A similar question might be asked about the value of an idea not effectively communicated to someone else. The answer would be much the same.

The objective of this book is to help you ensure that the ideas you have do generate all the impact they merit. What is more, if you become a particularly effective communicator, the impact of your ideas could even be greater than their intrinsic merit alone might otherwise allow.

Most of the benefits of such skill are self-evident. First of all, by communicating more effectively with the people around you, you make your life easier, richer and more enjoyable. There is a unique and abiding pleasure in carefully and persuasively phrasing a line of reasoning and then watching someone else's eyes light up with comprehension and active agreement.

Just as important, an effectively communicated idea then assumes a life of its own. It is transmitted—equally effectively, you hope—to become an active ingredient in achieving a greater good. Along the way, it will no doubt change somewhat (and perhaps even improve) as other intelligences are brought to bear on its existence. But nevertheless, the core of the idea remains yours. Then, like the parent of a child who grows to achieve greatness, you can revel in the satisfaction of creation.

If all of that holds true for effective face-to-face communication of the most basic sort, think what power a well-presented idea can have when it is put before tens of thousands, or hundreds of thousands or even millions of people simultaneously. That is where skill in media communication assumes its importance.

The mass media, by definition, can magnify the significance of any notion. Its power for good—and occasionally for evil—is awesome. For that reason, it should not be approached lightly. Effective communication bears with it a considerable degree of responsibility. After all, your message—whether it be reported in a magazine or newspaper or conveyed via the electronic media direct to any number of receptive listeners or viewers—can influence an incalculable number of people in their attitudes and even in their actions. You will have to live with any such consequences.

Does that mean that you should regard the idea of getting your ideas across to the masses with trepidation? Not at all.

For one, as you will discover in the following pages, long-term effective communication must have a basis in truth, particularly where the electronic media are concerned. That is not to say that all you see and hear in a broadcast is necessarily the truth, the whole truth and nothing but the truth. Far from it. But the microphone and the camera do have an uncanny knack for picking up anything of questionable veracity, particularly in the relatively free and easy atmosphere of Western broadcasting. The outright lie, the half-truth, and even the apparently harmless fib all tend to be emphasized and highlighted by the technological processes involved in bouncing a voice and an image from a studio into space and back again into your sitting room.

As for broadcasting in a less easy-going milieu, recent events in Eastern Europe have proven that a medium dominated by decades of lies and half-truths has little if any power of mass persuasion. Its *de facto* role in such societies is more to enhance the oppressors' self-esteem than to disinform with any degree of effectiveness.

Therefore, with the comfort of knowing that all you are doing on television is conveying the truth as you perceive it, any fears of being caught out, of being exposed as a video charlatan should be put from your mind for good.

Instead, this book has been written to help you concentrate on how to make the best of any communications opportunity that might arise. As you might expect, it begins with the fundamentals. At times, and particularly in the earlier chapters, these pages might read like a celebration of the obvious.

Be patient.

That which appears obvious seldom really is. It might be there, right before your eyes like a chameleon on the bark of a tree, but until its precise contours are pointed out, it remains invisible.

Fortunately, your patience should not be stretched too far. One of the first things you will have noticed about this book is its size. It is what publishers euphemistically call 'a slim volume'. This was intentional. After all, if the authors can't get their own message across as quickly and simply as possible, they can hardly expect you to cut through the verbosity and obfuscation that plague most communication attempts.

Given this book's brevity—and having read thus far—make the commitment to read it all the way through in as few sittings as possible. On a first reading, resist the temptation to skip to those chapters or sections you think might be most immediately useful. Without the grounding of the pages that come before, you might well miss out on an essential practice or principle and, as a result, fall flat on your face when you can least afford to assume that less than dignified posture.

Instead, start from the beginning and move as planned from the generalities to the specifics of communication skills. Then, when you have mastered those, you will move on to the big time: to television itself, with which about half of this book is directly concerned.

Once you have done that, and if all goes according to the writers' plans, something special should happen. Though the first chapters, which deal with more mundane media, were designed to give you the proper grounding to approach the highly specialized demands of television, you will find that the opposite also holds true. Once your mastery of telecommunications is achieved, your performance in all of the other communications disciplines suddenly takes off as well. Your letters, your memos, your speeches and your presentations take on a new tone of relaxed assurance. Not only are the externals of their presentation improved, but you will also find that the ideas generating these communications efforts in the first place have a greater incisiveness and clarity than ever before.

By understanding and putting into practice what you will read in the following pages, you will effectively change the way you think and, equally important, the way you get those thoughts across to others.

As a television director might warn an imminent subject for the camera's lens: 'You're on'—not merely next but now and for the rest of your life.

ACKNOWLEDGEMENT

Extract on pp. 122–130 from *the Bob Newhart Show* (episode entitled 'Mr X') © copyright MTM Entertainment. Adapted and reproduced by permission of MTM Entertainment.

1
On the receiving end

In which you will initially learn to become aware of the infinite variety of communications around you. Then, by kick-starting your long-dormant critical facility, you begin to understand why some communications are effective while others prove to be a waste of time, effort and money. By the end of the chapter, you will no longer accept any communication at face value. Your perception of the world around you will be akin to that of a patient who has just undergone successful surgery for cataracts. Suddenly, everything will seem crystalline and almost painfully fresh in its clarity. This altered state of perception is, you will discover, something to be cherished and cultivated. It is the first step on the road to effective communications.

Look around you.

Listen.

The world is one immense transmitter, constantly beaming countless competing messages in your direction.

You are the receiver.

Some messages are on your wavelength; others are lost to the ozone. Of the messages you do receive, some have an immediate impact. Others are more insidious, taken in subliminally and only gradually influencing your thought processes. But most of the messages sent in your direction are—for one reason or another—simply ignored. There is, after all, a limit to what your senses can absorb.

Think about it. While you are reading this book—these very words—your mind is (or should be) attuned to its meaning. Influencing your perception of this volume are purely physical characteristics: the typestyle in which these words are set; the way in which the text is laid out on the page; the colour, weight and texture of the paper on which these words appear.

On another level, the vocabulary, the sentence structure, the rhetorical devices, the punctuation and the overall tone have an important bearing on whether or not you will continue to read beyond this paragraph. What is more, if you do decide to go on, they will influence the way in which you proceed.

Apart from those messages internal to the book, there are any number of external signals competing for your attention. If you are at home, the television in the next room might well be tuned to a raucous aerobic exercise session on the morning slot, or the relentless beat of the latest pop video, or the drone of your daily horoscope or news of the latest developments in the Middle East.

Meanwhile, on the breakfast table before you, a packet of bran flakes loudly and proudly proclaims its high fibre content and miraculous impact on your digestive tract. And on the radio that always seems to be playing somewhere in the house during the morning rush, you might be tuned in to the latest farming bulletin.

Or, suppose you are reading this book during a lunch break at the office. You're sitting back comfortably, feet on desk. Even with the most attentive of intents, your eyes are bound to stray sooner or later to the PC flickering at your workstation, insistently displaying the tables of last month's sales figures. (Perhaps not as good as they could have been?)

Even on the commuter train your concentration is hostage to your environment: if you are lucky, the guard will be announcing in his usual inaudible way the reason for the quarter-hour delay, while the scent worn by the woman in the adjacent seat is conveying its own insistent story and distracting you from the message on this page. It happens all the time.

No matter what the environment, the static caused by all those simultaneous, competing channels of communication—each determined that its own message will get through—would soon drive even the most receptive minded to overload and possibly into insanity.

Advertising provides a prime example. Some of the century's most creative minds, over-stimulated by lingering over the longest lunches in history, constantly conspire to get you to buy their clients' goods and services. That's their job and they are nothing if not persistent. Media analysts estimate that by the time you reach the age of 21, you have been exposed to as many as *2 million* advertising messages. With maturity and increasing affluence, exposure to advertising will inevitably increase thereafter.

It is a daunting realization. But congratulations are in order. You have so far survived all that expert sensory and intellectual bombardment. A bit bloodied, perhaps, but relatively solvent and with judgement more or less unimpaired. How have you managed it?

Knowingly or not, you have filtered out the maddening cacophony beamed at you during every waking hour of every day. At best, you are oblivious to the largest proportion of the noise. Most of the rest you can relegate to a not unpleasant background hum. At any given time, only a few of the messages beamed in your direction actually do get through.

Which ones? And why?

To continue with the opening analogy: though you are indeed a receiver, your role is by no means entirely passive. You have in your control a fine-tuning mechanism. It is a most effective means of defence: the critical faculty.

You decide—more often than not unconsciously—what is worth listening to, thinking about and then perhaps acting upon. What you probably do *not* do is analyse which elements of the message have brought you to those unconscious conclusions.

This is hardly surprising. After all, though from your earliest infancy you have been responding to human communications stimuli, you hardly ever exercised the discipline required to *analyse* those stimuli. You were simply never taught to do so. It is the rare child who, when asked *why* he enjoys a favourite video or *why* she wants a revoltingly pastel shaded plastic pony featured in a particular television commercial, can supply simple and cogent reasons for a particular impulsive desire. 'Why do you want that?' 'I just do' is almost invariably the extent of the verbal exchange between beleaguered parent and petulant offspring.

Give or take a few syllables, the adult answer to the same sort of question is likely to be similar. After a party political broadcast, for example, you might nod sagely in quiet and confident concurrence with the party luminary you have just seen. Or—more likely perhaps—the broadcast leaves you incoherent with rage. Whatever the reaction, chances are you accept it for what it is and file it away to form part of the mental dossier we all keep on national political figures.

This is understandable. But it is also a waste of a hidden and highly useful talent.

Every communication effort—be it a formal memo from your managing director, a slick television slot or a scrawled note left on your pillow—has a surface meaning, of course. But beneath that, and contributing to its overall effect are dozens of smaller clues, cues, hints and subtexts. Mood, tone, style, syntax, vocabulary, emphases, pauses, punctuation are all individually and collectively contributing to both the meaning and the effectiveness of any message that you receive.

You perceive these ingredients, but seldom make any attempt to isolate them: to determine how they contribute to your overall perception of the communication effort. Of course, it could be argued that these details do not matter. What is important is the message itself, not the manner in which it is conveyed. And perhaps that *should* be true.

But the intermediate stages in achieving that truth are often much more interesting than the truth itself. The enjoyment of good food provides a useful analogy. When presented with a delicious new dish at a restaurant, part of the fun is in savouring and identifying those herbs and spices and techniques that make the recipe so distinctive. Or, conversely, there is a certain pedantic pleasure in being able to discern exactly what is missing from a less satisfactory dish: how browning the meat might have sparked its flavour or a sprinkling of cayenne could have elevated your dish of ragout from the banal to the intriguing.

Of course, it takes a well-developed palate to exercise such discrimination. The gastronome achieves this by *conscious* exposure to as many varied taste sensations as possible. The drawback to this constant exercising of the critical faculty—whether it be of food or communications—is the time factor. Discernment comes with knowledge and experience, and neither of those can be acquired over-night. But there is a consolation. The process itself, the slow, steady and deliberate application, exercise and stretching of your own critical judgement can become a fascinating and entertaining pastime.

Consider the possibilities.

For one, you need never be bored again. How often have you sat through one of those interminable meetings that seem to be an inescapable part of doing business? Perhaps, for a bit of light relief, the planning manager is doing a slide presentation of market forecasts. As an intelligent employee on whose prosperity these figures could well have major significance, these figures provide a potentially fascinating and vital subject. Yet you find your eyes are glazing over. You try shifting your attention to the doodle on your pad, which is already rivalling a medieval illuminated manuscript in its elaboration and so attracting a raised eyebrow from your neighbour. Or, if you're really desperate, you might resort to the foolproof technique of slowing pressing the fingernails of one hand into the palm of the other. It's a gory trick, but invariably effective in keeping you awake, if grimacing.

How much more profitable, though, to turn the situation to your advantage. Study the hapless planning manager. What is he doing wrong? Why is he talking in that soporific monotone? Is he speaking to you, or reading from his notes? Does he catch your eye as he drones on? Or does he keep his attention firmly fixed on the screen? And what is he showing you? Is all of it really relevant? Do you need to see these slides? Are they clear and concise, simultaneously encapsulating and reinforcing his message? Do they capture the graphic spirit of your organization? Or, more probable, are they illegible, crammed with extraneous information and sloppily, if expensively, executed?

Once you have kick-started your critical faculty by asking yourself such questions, even the most terminally tedious of meetings to which you are subjected can suddenly become a valuable educational experience.

But don't stop there. Delve further. Be vicious. Ask yourself why he is retreating into the security of phrases heavy with departmental jargon. Can't he get his ideas across in simple English, or is his use of obfuscating language more sinister? What is he trying to put over to you? What is he trying to hide?

Get personal. Must he slouch? Surely he doesn't have to stand with his hands apparently glued together in the position of a cricket box. And how are you supposed to take him seriously when he is sporting a tie like that?

Once you get into the habit, it is difficult to stop. And why should you?

Having started with meetings, expand your critical skills. Start mining the mother lode of your in-tray. It should provide incomparable riches in the form of pompous letters, ambiguous, time-wasting memoranda and rambling reports.

It is all great and illuminating fun. But what does this exercise have to do with effective use of the media which is, after all, the topic of this book?

In the mid-1960s, a Canadian academic, Marshall McLuhan, shot to fame with his analysis of the importance of television. Central to his thesis, as set out in his most celebrated book, *The Medium is the Message* (1967), was the impact of the media on our methods of perception. Focusing primarily on broadcasting, he pointed out that television and the information it conveys coexist in a form of symbiosis. On screen, what you say becomes inextricably linked with the way in which you say it. Perform well, and the content of your message comes across in a positive way. Perform badly, and your message—no matter how worthy or interesting or vital—is subverted.

More than 20 years ago, McLuhan's theories were startling in their impact. And, perhaps inevitably, McLuhan himself became something of a media star, appearing in a steady stream of documentaries, chat shows and even—in a memorable cameo spot—on the 1960s comedy show, *Laugh-In*. All in all, the situation was irresistible in its neatness: an internationally acclaimed guru of the television age used the medium he had analysed to spread his message about that medium. His success vividly proved the validity of his ideas. Yet ironically at the same time, the intellectual significance of McLuhan's thesis was subsumed by the power of the medium he celebrated.

Since McLuhan's time, the power of television has been universally recognized. It is hardly surprising that this book does not tackle the effective use of this most potent of all the media in its first three chapters. You have to learn to walk before you can run.

Does that mean that you are currently incapable of effective communication? Not at all. You are obviously doing some things right. But which? That is what you need to know. You also need to know why those techniques work. And why others do not.

If that means going back to the basics of business communications, so much the better. Corporate life is far too hectic to waste your time producing ineffective—or worse still, counterproductive—memos, letters, presentations, or speeches.

Expertise gained in these disciplines will carry you onward to the trickier bits: the ordeal of the employee forum, the potential pitfalls of the press release. Then the going gets tougher still, with press conferences and radio interviews. Finally, you will have the grounding and confidence to approach the most effective—and the most damaging—communication tool of all: television.

Then something extraordinary will happen. Once you have mastered television, joining the ranks of video blessed, everything will fit into place. Though different skills and techniques are employed, your proficiency in the more basic disciplines will become more pronounced. What is more, as you become better at getting your ideas across, you will actually enjoy exercising your persuasive communications skills.

2
Just who do you think you are?

In which you will take a giant step further in effective communications. Criticizing others and their efforts is a relatively easy—and usually thoroughly enjoyable—pastime. Turning your critical faculties inward is something else entirely. Self-dissection is, after all, a bizarre exercise. It engenders emotions reminiscent of the way you felt at school when your biology instructor insisted that you take your own blood sample. It is highly difficult to remain detached when drawing your own blood. Yet detachment is precisely what is required. And the first step in achieving that detachment is by answering the question posed by the chapter title.

By now you have acquired the habit of looking critically at the communications efforts of those around you. You have become merciless in your disdain, discriminating in your praise. You are beginning to see which messages work for you, which do not and—most important of all—why.

Such an outlook carries with it a heady sense of potency. After all, some pretty high-powered communication experts are out to persuade you how to think and so influence your action. Your new-found critical faculty should provide an effective fortification against their pervasive and sometimes even insidious weapons.

But beware. There is a potential drawback to the critical—and even moral—high ground you now occupy. It can make you insufferably complacent and conceited.

To avoid those perils—and to move a step closer toward media mastery yourself—now is the time to acquire a much more difficult skill. Having learnt to criticize the communication efforts of others, you must now turn the weapon on yourself, putting your own words and actions under close and occasionally quite painful scrutiny.

The only way to do this is to acquire yet another new point of view. In the first chapter you were asked to hone your senses, to become, in effect, a critically-aware receiver. Now you must do the reverse. You must step outside yourself and analyse your own role as a transmitter of messages. To do that, you must develop a vital sense of detachment. It is only by achieving this sense of detachment, this otherness, that you can acquire the vital facility for *self*-criticism.

First, however, you must answer this question: What is self?

There is no easy reply, at least without then getting bogged down in the psychoanalytical technicalities of ego and id. In any case, there probably is no one answer. You are many different—and probably even contradictory—things to different people. What is more, you behave accordingly.

To your parents you are forever their offspring: innocent, vulnerable and the object of uncritical love no matter what you might do or say. To your children you are the first figure of authority, to be either obeyed or defied: the individual, against whom all other authority figures in their lives will be measured. Your spouse, depending on mood and situation, sees you as lover, friend, fellow-inmate, gaoler, breadwinner, spendthrift, housekeeper, bookkeeper, host, gardener, plumber, decorator, electrician or layabout. To your subordinates at work you are one person: aloof, perhaps—maybe even tyrannical—and with a notorious obsession with petty detail. To your superiors you might be an entirely different creature: eager and ambitious, but maybe a bit slipshod. And as far as your peers in the office are concerned, you can be a co-operative colleague or an immovable obstacle; a firm ally or an untrustworthy competitor.

Each of these people in your life has a different and varying perception of you. Though you might find their analyses amusing, disturbing or even shocking, each is correct in his or her perception because, after all, that perception is based on the signals that you yourself have given them, as well as on your ideas and actions. Yet if someone in one of these categories of acquaintance were to describe your character to an individual from another of your social circles, it is doubtful that anything approaching a recognizable picture would emerge.

Which, then, is the real you?

The answer to that searching question is probably obvious by now: all of them and none of them. And to communicate effectively, you must come to grips with that paradox. That paradox, in turn, leads inevitably to another set of questions. How do the people around you arrive at these conflicting sets of conclusions? Are you really such an erratic figure?

The answer to that last question must be in the affirmative. But then you have the consolation of knowing that everyone else is at least equally erratic in personality variation.

If you think about it, none of this comes as any real surprise. You have been at least partially conscious of these dichotomies for a very long time. Think about the varying standards of behaviour you have applied since early childhood. According to your mother, your table manners at home no doubt left something to be desired. But at a party, or under the scrutiny of a friend's parents, your standards of courtesy seemed to improve spontaneously and effortlessly. Similarly, at school, the language you used among your classmates was probably a good deal more colourful and less grammatical than the carefully chosen words you uttered when summoned to the headteacher's study to discuss a misdemeanour. These alterations in behaviour and speech patterns were not the result of hypocrisy. They were merely an implicit understanding of which response would be most appropriate—and effective—in a given situation. Just as an airline captain turns on the automatic pilot and is confident that the plane will respond to varying conditions, you tend to trust in your brain's mechanism to determine correct and effective behaviour in a wide range of constantly shifting situations.

When, for one reason or another, this does not occur, problems arise. George Bernard Shaw's most popular comedy, *Pygmalion*, is a study in inappropriate behaviour and communication. In the play's most famous scene, the Cockney heroine, Eliza Doolittle, forgets her altered surroundings and scandalizes a London drawing room by interjecting in the midst of her awkwardly polite smalltalk the fatal word 'bloody'. This raises the play's biggest laugh. Yet there is a tragic dimension to the work, as well, and this rests in the hero's complete inability to communicate on anything other than a syntactically impeccable basis. At one point, Henry Higgins pridefully proclaims his misguided consistency of manner: 'I address a duchess as though she were a flower girl; a flower girl as though she were a duchess', he insists. One of the ironies of the play is that though Higgins is a master of elocution, fiercely committed to teaching Eliza Doolittle the niceties of polite speech, his own communications skills are fundamentally disastrous. Ultimately, his impeccable pronunciation of his abhorrent philosophy of human relations—delivered just when a modicum of conciliation would win the companionship he craves—leaves him bereft by the fall of the final curtain.

What Higgins never bothers to do is assess the impact of his speech—in terms of either content or style—on his listeners. He is too selfish, too self-absorbed, too conceited to bother and so pays for these faults with the loss of his Eliza.

Higgin's tragic flaw can be categorized as a total lack of empathy. He is simply incapable of stepping into anyone else's shoes. Consequently, his point of view, his frame of reference, is restricted to the dangerously narrow confines of his own senses. He suffers from an emotional form of tunnel vision.

Empathy is nothing short of a moral imperative, the quality that brings the golden rule to life. It is also, not coincidentally, the basis of effective communication. What is more, you already practise empathy to at least some practical extent every day.

It is 7.00 am and you are dressing for work. Today your schedule calls for attendance at the weekly management meeting. As you are getting dressed do you reach for the slightly hairy tweeds, or the midnight blue pinstripes? It is probably not even a conscious decision that makes you opt for the more conservative, more obviously businesslike choice. Everyone—you included—would simply feel much more comfortable seeing you in traditional business garb, and you do not want to discomfort your colleagues, or your bosses, do you? (Nor do you want them to regard you as the odd one out, but that is another, though coexisting impulse.) On an admittedly very minor scale, your sartorial decision is empathy at work.

Like courtesy, empathy makes life go more smoothly. In fact, it is only in the absence of empathy, those moments when the concept of self comes to the forefront and dominates your thoughts and actions, that problems tend to arise. How often have you heard yourself saying exactly the wrong thing in a conversation? No doubt you did not mean to offend, but suddenly, even as you were mouthing the fatal words, you knew the consequences. Why? Because your empathetical instinct once again came to the fore, if a bit too late to put right your *faux pas*.

Empathy is a habit. And like any habit—good or bad—it can be acquired. When next watching a drama on television or film, put yourself in the part of the protagonist. Do not merely sympathize with the character's predicament. Ask yourself how you would really *feel* in the same situation. Given those feelings, how would you react? Not only will this exercise heighten your interest and enjoyment in the drama, it will also expand your own range of consciousness.

Or, go one step further. Actors are by definition effective communicators. It is their job to move you to a whole spectrum of emotions, including laughter, tears, horror and joy. To do that, they must either have or acquire an understanding of how those emotional states are achieved. One way they accomplish this is through a technique pioneered earlier this century by Stanislawski in the Moscow Art Theatre and later developed by Lee Strassberg at his Actors' Studio in New York. It came to be known as 'The Method'. This involves concentrating on your own sensory memories to summon up a genuine emotional response to a specific situation.

For instance, at work suppose you are faced with the unpleasant task of telling a subordinate that his or her performance is substandard. Do not imagine how *he* or *she* will respond to your criticisms. Think back to your *own* response to criticism. How did you feel? Was there a hot flush of blood to your face? Did your palms sweat? Did your eyes begin to water? Did you develop tremors in the arms or legs? Did you feel guilty? Or angry? Or ashamed? Or misunderstood? Or threatened? Did your voice develop a tremor? What happened to your posture? Suddenly, you are experiencing something akin to your earlier distress all over again. That is empathy as achieved through 'The Method'.

Naturally, an actor trained in this technique carries it further, and actually manages to reproduce those feelings in the context of the script. You need not (and without proper training and genuine acting talent probably could not and should not) go that far. All you have to do is use those feelings you have summoned as the basis for dealing with any real-life scene in which you find yourself.

Returning to the task at hand, what is the best way to deal with this recalcitrant employee? Empathize, and use empathy in every aspect of the interaction.

First, set the scene. The employee's workplace, or your office? Or perhaps over lunch or on other neutral ground? And when should it take place? As you know from your own empathetical exercise, the timing of such a confrontation can have a major bearing on its impact. So can the body language employed: face to face across a desk, side by side on a sofa, standing up and looking down from a height advantage—each has its own particular meaning. A desk encounter is remote and formal; a sofa discussion is friendly and intimate; a height advantage is as intimidating as it is no doubt meant to be.

And what should be the result of your meeting? Naturally, you have to temper your messages accordingly. Do you want to stimulate your employee to do more and better work? Or do you want to let him or her know that further performances of a substandard nature could mean he or she is out of a job? Do you want to appear sympathetic? Or would long-suffering disappointment on your part be a more judicious sentiment to get across? The possibilities are virtually limitless, but effective use of empathy can help you arrive at the message—or combination of messages—that will be most effective in achieving the outcome you are after. What is more, you have the assurance that the meeting should hold few if any surprises for you—assuming, of course, that your exercise in empathy was complete.

What will be surprising is how useful this skill can become—not merely at work, but in every facet of life. The combined ability to stand outside yourself—that elusive quality of detachment—and then to project your own psyche into the sensibilities of a fellow human being is a highly potent force. Unlike some other potent forces, however, its use is entirely laudable.

It is also a prerequisite for mastery in those other media skills that will expand your circle of influence from a single person across the room or office to millions of people across the nation or around the world.

That is a big step to take all at once. So the next chapter will concentrate on an intermediate achievement: the effective use of the traditional business communications tools.

3
Grasping the tools of the trade

Which takes a look at how you can combine your newly-honed, coolly self-critical sense of detachment with the warmth of your empathetical outreach within a typical office environment. The internal business media—the memo, the letter, the presentation, the speech, the employee forum, the employee newsletter—each has its potential benefits as well as its potential pitfalls. And each must be approached with a special blend of detachment, precision and empathy if it is to be productive.

No one can be considered a skilled craftsperson who does not have a complete mastery of the tools at hand. The carpenter's plane and awl; the mason's plumbline and square; the tailor's tape and needle—all of them require years of training and practice before their peculiar demands and subtleties become so familiar that they are second nature to the experts who wield them.

But what about the typical business executive? The communications tools available are certainly familiar enough. After all, everyone can write a letter or a memo or polish off a report to employees if sufficiently well versed on the subject. Or so everyone seems to think.

The result? It can be found in your in-tray at the start of every business day. The ambiguous memo, the infuriatingly pompous letter and the callous personnel announcement are no doubt all too familiar. But begin any critique of such communications disasters by calling into play your quality of empathy. Did your colleague who dashed off that memo actually intend to confuse you? Did the writer of the letter really mean to offend by his stuffy tone? And why on earth would the personnel officer want to stress—in writing, no less—her indifference to the plight of employees she is paid to keep happy?

More often than not, the authors of these unfortunate missives are victims of their own faulty communications skills. Unfortunately, they are not alone in churning out less than perfect bits of communication.

Having weeded through the contents of your in-tray, turn to your out-tray. What does it contain at 5.00 pm or thereabouts? Again, summon up all your powers of self-criticism and empathy and steel yourself for a less than pleasant revelation. In all honesty, is every piece of written communication you produced in the course of your busy business day guaranteed to have the effects you originally desired? Or—more likely—is the work you churned out about on a par with the rubbish you received?

Of course, there might be some consolation in being part of a crowd. But not much. And while corporate conformity does have its advocates, no one would argue that it is career enhancing to be the author of sloppy, counter-productive and perhaps even dangerously ambiguous or unintentionally offensive communications. That is why the following pages focus on some basic techniques to improve your performance in the most common of business media—both written and aural.

THE MEMO

This is the most basic, most widely used of written business media. After the simple phone call or—often better still, the welcome chance to wander down the hall for a chat—the memo is the easiest, least formal means of communication within an organization.

That, at any rate, is the theory.

In practice, the memo, whether scrawled by hand on a scrap of yellow paper, or precisely typewritten, checked and re-typed on your heaviest bond, is one of the trickiest of all business communication tools.

The risk factor rests precisely in the flexibility of the format itself. By definition nothing more—nor less—than a written reminder, the memo clearly sets out its topic and, in the course of what should be a lucid and concise text, makes its points. There is no room in a memo for the luxury of discursive waffle that a letter can afford.

The pared down simplicity of a well-written memo gives the form a remarkable purity. This purity, in turn, admirably sets off the thoughts that prompted the memo to be written in the first place. When you write a memo, think along the lines of a clean, spare traditional Japanese room. All it requires are the essentials: functionally and pleasingly arranged. Anything extraneous would be glaringly, and worse still, embarrassingly, out of place. That's what a memo should be like. It seldom is.

Instead of a structure of Zen-like simplicity, the memo is more often a ramshackle affair, a maze of half-conceived notions, loosely linked, that neither inform the reader nor initiate action. Sometimes, the memo contains no ideas at all. Instead, it is used by the writer solely for his or her own benefit, to serve as a kind of rear-guard line of defence in low-grade corporate skirmishes. As such it is worse than useless to its recipient. It is a bore, violating the cardinal rule of effective communications. It wastes the recipient's (or, more typically, since the writer of poor memos tends to copy in anyone and everyone he or she can think of, the *recipients'*) time.

But the memo as a communications form has its own potent revenge. The very nature of the medium's direct simplicity cruelly exposes the writer's every flaw. A badly written memo, probably more than any other communication, tends to rebound on its author. Even a simple announcement of good news, the sort of memo that is always welcome to the recipient, can backfire.

Consider this classic, which was written to prepare managers in a brewing conglomerate about an informal, but nevertheless traditional, extra half-day's holiday for employees on Christmas Eve:

This is to inform you that it is custom and practice for employees to finish at lunchtime on Christmas Eve.

To avoid impacting other units this will not be announced in writing.

Best wishes.

An announcement in writing that something will not be announced in writing does little to sustain either the author's credibility or dignity. Yet the originator of that memorable little memo is probably an intelligent and possibly even a literate individual. How, then, does he manage to come across as a bureaucratic bungler?

Let's take a look at the pitfalls you might encounter every time you decide that a memo is called for.

First of all, ask yourself what you hope to achieve by addressing, on paper, either an individual colleague or several associates at once. Are you certain that you couldn't accomplish the same objective—more easily, more quickly, more cost efficiently—simply by picking up the telephone?

Having determined that what you have to say genuinely deserves the dignity of the written word, stick to that resolution. Write the memo yourself. Do not give in to the deluded grandeur of dictation, either directly or through the use of a dictaphone.

Effective dictation is a skill little short of genius. And even geniuses usually get it wrong. In mid-career the novelist Henry James decided to give up direct work on manuscripts and so employed a secretary to record his prose. Though James's unique talent for psychological insight and character motivation remained unchanged, his novels became, for the most part, purgatory to read. They needlessly burdened his audience with endless, tortuous sentences rendered virtually incomprehensible under the weight of highly complex, interwoven subsidiary clauses. Meaning fell victim to mere complexity of punctuation.

Does doing this initial work yourself take any longer? No longer than it needs to. Writing your own memos exerts a powerful discipline and a just reward. You must organize your thoughts and, having done so, it is in your own best interests to express those thoughts as quickly as possible—if only to free your time to move on to another task.

And if writing in long hand ultimately proves to be too onerous, bite the bullet and take a course in keyboard skills. In an age in which few desks are without a personal computer, a month or two of minor humiliation on a proper typing course will pay dividends in years of enhanced and improved productivity.

Do not, however, confuse any newly acquired keyboard skills with automatic prose proficiency. One drawback to producing your own typescript or computer-generated copy is its professional appearance. After all, a neatly laid out, thoroughly spell-checked document does have a certain finesse. It looks authoritative. In this, as in all things, appearances can deceive. Such deception can be particularly dangerous when it involves electronic mail, which is an increasingly common workplace innovation.

Electronic mail urges its user to live up to the speed of its own digital impulses. You come in every morning, switch on your PC and check the in-tray flashing up in quick succession on your screen. There is something inevitably cold and remote about the process which, by its very nature, seems to encourage an immediate response in similar style. The result: a peculiar impersonal quality reflected in the tone of the messages it carries. In the rather weird flickering blue or green light of a VDU, it is all too easy to forget that there is (or should be) a human being at the other end of the system. Perhaps that is why the contents of electronic mail tend to be even less well thought out and more sloppily written than the contents of a conventional in-tray.

To avoid this danger, do not give in to the temptation of immediate response to any electronic mail. Let the system wait. Read over your correspondence and formulate an immediate reply, by all means. But resist the temptation to send the memo. Instead, go on to do something else. Then, later, when the opportunity arises, re-read the electronic memo you received and then re-read your response.

In fact, it makes sense applying this delaying tactic to any memo you write, whether electronically or conventionally. Having produced the first draft, put it aside. Or, better still, keep a permanent tray or box file on your desk in which to place *all* written work. Once it is there, leave it alone for a while. Let it mature. Move on to other work if time permits. Then, in half an hour or longer, go back to your draft and read it afresh. Use all your critical and empathetical skills and go through this catechism:

- What did you want to say in the memo?
- Does the memo actually convey this message?
- Is the message clear?
- Is your argument cogent?
- Does the memo have any unintentional undertones in style or content?

- What will your reader or readers make of the message?
- Is their understanding what you intended them to know?
- Will they understand what, if anything, you want them to do in response?
- Does your memo instil in its recipients either a desire to do your bidding or an understanding that it would be in their best interests to do so? (Not to be confused with a threat.)

And the clincher of the catechism:

- What would *you* do if you were the recipient of this memo rather than its sender?

No memo should leave your desk—or your PC—until you can satisfactorily answer each and every one of these questions. Then, and only then, can you be confident that the memos you send will do their job *for* you rather than do a job *on* you.

THE LETTER

A business letter is a much weightier document than a memo. For one, it is almost invariably external. Therefore, it appears, usually on premium bond, beneath the full majesty of your business letterhead. Given those dignified appurtenances, your letter becomes a quasi-official document. It speaks not only for you but also for your company. There is a double-edged quality to this status. On the one hand, you—and your ideas—benefit from the clout of the organization behind you. The drawback is equally obvious. A badly worded missive not only embarrasses you personally, but also rebounds on the people who pay your salary. That is worth remembering next time you are tempted to tear off a quick response.

Though the letter is, by its very nature, a more formal document, the mental disciplines it demands are similar to those required by the memo. Before setting pen to paper (or, with your hard work on the typing course behind you, fingers to keyboard) first of all ask yourself why you are doing this.

As with the memo, could the message you are about to impart be better conveyed over the telephone or in person? If the message is still to be in letter form, then go on with what should by now be the next familiar question: exactly what is it you want to say? Are you informing, persuading or attempting to do both? Is this letter the start of a correspondence or are you responding to an earlier communication? Naturally, the answers to these questions should have a direct and inevitable bearing on the style and tone of your text.

Next, get back into your empathetical mode. To whom are you writing? What will he or she make of the information and the way in which you are conveying it? Is your correspondent older and more senior than you, or younger and more junior? Have you met or written to one another before? If so, does this bear a reminder in your text or is the previous correspondence either irrelevant or perhaps best left unmentioned?

As for style, it is much too individual a thing on which to pontificate. Beyond the requirements for cogency, clarity and brevity (for your own benefit as well as that of your correspondent), style is up to you and your perceptions of the person to whom you are writing. That being said, there are some cautions to bear in mind. For one, try at all costs to avoid the empty phrase. Admittedly, any communication form that dictates the use of 'dear' as a greeting and 'yours truly' or 'sincerely yours' or—worse still perhaps—'yours faithfully' as a valediction can have a hollow ring. But those are the conventions under which letters are written. Console yourself with the knowledge that letters in English at least escape the more flowery phrases endemic to letters in French and Italian. In English we are fortunate in being able to keep the hackneyed to a just bearable minimum. Therefore, do not give in to the lazy temptation to pad your prose with such other ringing, usually archaic pomposities as:

'Please find enclosed . . .'

'Further to my letter of . . .'

'In reply to yours of the — instant . . .'

'I hope this letter finds you in the best of health . . .'

The cringe-making list could go on and on. Yet avoiding these empty formulae is easy. No matter what type of letter you are writing, simply use your own words to express your own thoughts in as clear and original a way as possible.

One last stylistic caution: unless you are already a fully qualified lawyer, do not attempt to write like one. Even if you are one, ask yourself if the particular letter you are writing really should be couched in the language of your profession. Admittedly, a letter to an outside organization could have an impact on any future legal dispute. But if that consideration were to rule all your actions, you would never accomplish anything anyway. Instead, when it comes to correspondence, rely on clear, simple prose to express your own good intentions—and then hope for the best.

Once you have produced a letter, follow the same safeguards as those employed on the memo. Put it aside. Let it fester a bit. And then subject yourself to the identical catechism before finally signing off and consigning your work to the inspection of its recipient.

EMPLOYEE COMMUNICATIONS

Employees are invariably told by their superiors—in memos, announcements, bulletins and newsletters—that they are their company's most important asset. It is a pleasant sentiment, warm and cosy. But it is also often patently untrue. Employees are the first to sense this, which is hardly surprising considering the quality of the communications aimed in their direction by a complacent management.

Consider the following message incorporated in the end-of-year issue of a West Country construction company's employee publication. The piece was, it should be pointed out, the managing director's own work—of which he was no doubt proud.

> Christmas, as we all know, is a time for reflection as well as a time to look forward to the year ahead. A time to take stock and agree priorities, so I thought I'd take the opportunity to do a little bit of this myself.

So far, so banal. But it gets more interesting.

> A year ago we were still really getting our act together as a company. There were still a few people in the company who really didn't want to progress and go forward; they wanted to keep the company in a static status quo, almost stagnant position. These people are no

longer around and, whilst during the last 12 months we've probably had more than our fair share of turnover in staff, I think we came through it all to be much stronger with a clearer focus on our future—more team-orientated, non-political and certainly we now have a true company culture and a defined forward plan . . .

Involving an even higher rate of staff dismissals and enforced redundancies perhaps? With such cosy tidings of comfort and joy at the holiday season, it is not difficult to imagine the level of empathetic employee communication during times of the year less noted for their conviviality.

In communicating with employees, management must take into account two fundamentals: first of all, thanks to the effectiveness of the grapevine, there is little you can tell your employees that they do not already know—at least in sketchy form. Is there a merger approaching, a round of redundancies, a significant change in benefits? Employees will be on to the general idea as soon as you yourself know, and perhaps even before. Therefore, speed in employee communications is essential. You have to get your official story out before the unofficial story—over which you have no control—becomes accepted as gospel.

Secondly, using your empathetic impulse, put yourself in an employee's place. You are at work, probably 40 hours a week, 48 weeks a year, spending a goodly chunk of your life performing tasks that you would not normally choose to undertake; and all for one reason—you need the money. Under those circumstances, you are obliged to leave the comfort of your home at an unearthly hour almost every day of the year and then take instructions, orders and even reprimands from someone to whom, under other, more just circumstances, you might not even care to give the time of day. Nevertheless, expedience dictates that you are there, day in and day out. Moreover, it is virtually a life sentence, without parole. If you leave your job, for whatever reason, the most you can look forward to is another, rather similar job until that day a long way off when you retire on a no doubt less-than-adequate pension.

Is it any wonder, then, that the typical employee is perhaps somewhat less than gruntled, and regards any form of official executive communication with a degree of scepticism? Just think of your own reactions when confronted with the usual head-office doublespeak. Why, unless your own employee communications are radically different, should messages from you be perceived any more positively?

One way to achieve this rare credibility among employees is to *recognize* that natural scepticism and *turn it to your advantage*. The technique is admittedly somewhat tricky. First, you must have the confidence to take yourself and your business lightly. You must also have some confidence in and respect for your employees. Only then is it advisable to indulge in *selective iconoclasm*.

Company journals in particular benefit from this approach. A tone of amused, ironic detachment can effectively chronicle most aspects of your business at least some of the time. When employees hear, via the grapevine, of missed opportunities, botched repairs, and misdirected deliveries and then see these mild misfortunes amusingly and accurately reported in their newsletter, management credibility soars. So long as specific employees themselves are not mentioned as the scapegoats in these reports, no one is hurt. And those employees who actually work to put right the errors—and are reported as doing so—consequently receive the peer and management recognition they deserve.

But that is only a secondary benefit. More important is the contagious nature of such candour. If you are seen as being highly believable in your treatment of minor matters, you will also be believed on the more important subjects. In conveying information on major topics humour is usually, but not invariably, out of place. What is really required is plain writing, making liberal use of direct action verbs in relatively simple sentence forms. Compare this example of less than empathetically announced news . . .

> In light of less than favourable third quarter results, it has been determined that a temporary scale-down of line operations could be efficacious until the current industry over-supply situation has been rectified. To this end, the relevant employees have been notified of the temporary half-time scheduling under which they will operate until further notice.

. . . with this version of the same information:

The entire industry is facing a product glut at the moment. A drop in our third quarter results gives tangible proof of the problem. As a temporary solution, the company has regretfully switched some lines to half-time operation. At the same time, however, the sales team is making a renewed effort to clear product backlog. Then, they will redouble their efforts to make sure that no matter what the market conditions, it won't be our products, or our people, who suffer.

Even though both paragraphs convey the same less than up-beat message, it is fairly clear which of the two leaves the employee simultaneously better informed and better motivated. In the final analysis, a better informed and better motivated workforce is the objective of any employee communications programme.

THE PRESENTATION

According to a highly respected psychological survey which asked its participants to list their greatest fears in order of priority, death came second. Which came first? Standing up and speaking before an audience.

There are some sound physiological reasons for this common dread. The racing pulse, the sweaty palms, the pounding in your ears—all are the direct or indirect result of a rush of adrenalin. This is the same substance that your body triggers to prepare you for fight or flight. When the power of the adrenalin is properly harnessed, it gives you the intensity and power you need for effective performance. When it is out of control, it leaves you a nervous mess.

One way to control the flow of adrenalin is to control the situation itself. A presentation is, when all is said and done, merely a mechanism for conveying information. You, the presenter, presumably know more about your subject than does your audience. If not, you would not—or should not—be doing a presentation in the first place.

Therefore, if you are presenting some information in public, you clearly *must* be an expert. But do not let that go to your head. After all, your audience might well contain individuals who know nearly as much as you do—or maybe more. Alternatively, your audience might know nothing at all about your subject. Or maybe they are a mixed crowd. As presenter, it is your responsibility and no one else's to determine the make-up of your audience and to tailor your script accordingly. It is as grievous an error to overload an audience with esoterica as it is to insult them with too simple a presentation.

Furthermore, on the optimistic assumption that you *are* likely to be better informed about your subject than anyone else in the room, questions from your audience should hold no terror. All you need do is prepare for them in advance. First, using your newly acquired skill for critical detachment, review your text and then proceed to pick holes in it. Look for any flaws in your argument, any dodgy facts, any less than valid assumptions. Then, either correct them before you speak or—equally valid—be prepared to defend them if questions arise.

What questions? That is where empathy comes into the picture. Look at your text from the point of your audience and dozens of questions will spring to mind. If you cannot answer them to your satisfaction—and, more important, to what you empathize will be *their* satisfaction—do more homework. If you can cope with any questions effectively, there is no problem.

Having prepared your script to the appropriate audience level, and then bolstered your confidence by anticipating every conceivable—and even inconceivable—question, your next concern should be how best to get your message across. This is often the most crucial part of any presentation. Unfortunately, it is often the aspect that is totally ignored.

Think back to the presentations you have seen in the course of a business career. In fact, put your mind back even further to your experiences of school, college and university. How many times were you inspired? And why? What set those relatively few genuine learning experiences apart from the usual drone of speech or lecture? Knowledge of subject was certainly important, but there was also a sparkle in the way that knowledge was conveyed. There was, in fact, an element of show business that made you sit up and take notice from the start.

The Broadway lyricist Steven Sondheim succinctly set out the requirement with typical flair in his musical *Gypsy*. In one scene, a veteran striptease artiste coaches a novice with some challenging advice on how to succeed in her chosen profession:

> You can pull all the stops out,
> Till they call the cops out;
> Grind your behind till you're banned.
> But you gotta get a gimmick
> If you want to get a hand.

The veteran continues:

> You can sacrifice your sacro'
> Working in the back row;
> Bump in a dump till you're dead.
> Kid, you gotta get a gimmick,
> If you want to get ahead!

This is not to suggest that you begin a business presentation with a bit of bump and grind. However, it is imperative to get your audience's attention from the start, and then keep it.

One fairly simple technique is to begin your talk with a statement so outrageous, so contrary to what your audience expects, that the crash of jaws dropping to the floor becomes almost audible. Such an opening takes a degree of courage and aplomb to carry off, but when done properly it is unbeatable.

Another, less drastic method is to open with an analogy, parable or story that only gradually, but tellingly, brings you and your audience to the main topic of your talk. Your allusion can be drawn from your own experiences, literature, the Bible, television, cinema or even musical comedy (see above).

A dramatic visual can also serve as a highly effective attention grabber—which brings us to the subject of visual aids. Charts, slides, overhead projections, snippets of video can all enhance your presentation. But be warned. They cannot do your job for you. Too many presenters feel that all they have to do is cram slides and overheads with facts and merely talk their audience through them. It does not work. You might as well merely distribute the visuals as printed matter and let your audience go through them at their own pace.

Instead, regard visual aids as devices that help you, rather than your audience. Used judiciously, they can be valuable rest and reference points for the speaker as well as clarifiers for the audience. They help to break up and pace a long talk, and can usefully emphasize major points. They must not, however, be so overloaded with detail that they take the audience's attention away from you and your main message. Nothing can destroy a presentation so thoroughly as an audience obliged to strain and squint to make out the finer points of too complex a slide or overhead. You and the words you are saying are the primary reasons for everyone else's presence in the room. Remember that and you cannot go far wrong.

But are you really speaking during a presentation, or merely reading from your carefully prepared script? Experts disagree on which is the best method. But, in fact, the *only* method is the one that works for you. Provided you are thoroughly familiar with your topic, it does not really matter whether you use a complete script, an outline in either page or index card format, or even a few rough notes scrawled on the back of a shopping list. Or, if you are comfortable doing so, speak completely off the cuff.

The only technique to avoid completely is rote memory, with each word laboriously learnt by heart. Every presentation should have an air of spontaneity. In fact, the more spontaneous it appears the better, since nothing is more fascinating to watch than a live show that has the possibility of going wrong. Conversely, nothing is more deadly than an automatic recitation—unless of course the speaker is fatally distracted from his screed or suddenly and irrevocably dries up. Such performances are indeed memorable, but for all the wrong reasons.

Having determined which technique—script, notes, outline or off the cuff—is best for you, the next step is to practise endlessly. Subject your family, friends, pets and bathroom mirror to the myriad delights of your performance. The more you rehearse, the more comfortable you will be. The more comfortable you are with what you are saying, the more attention you can pay to how you are saying it.

What about spontaneity? Some people argue that they should not rehearse as often as suggested, since it would take the life out of their actual performance. It will not; and the argument is merely a rationale for laziness. As any professional actor can tell you, every performance of a play, no matter how long its run, has its own unique chemistry—a complex compound formula generated by performer and audience alike. No amount of role repetition or rehearsal can stop this from occurring. Therefore, when the time comes for you to do your presentation for real, don't worry. The spontaneity will be there, combined with the confidence you need to give a good performance.

Do not, however, let your spontaneity and enthusiasm run away with you. When making any presentation, gauge your speed. While the human brain *can* aurally comprehend some 500 words per minute, your listeners will not. Nor will they sit still for very long if . . . you . . . self-consciously . . . slow . . . your . . . speech . . . to . . . an . . . unnatural . . . pace. Instead, aim for about 200 words per minute, only marginally slower than the pace maintained during normal conversation.

In fact, the best way to regard your presentation *is* as normal conversation. No matter what the size of your audience, all you are doing is talking to a group of people. So make eye contact, just as you always do in real life. But be certain that once having established eye contact with one member of your audience, you then move on to another. This important procedure was unfortunately forgotten by a company chairman when presiding over a major event at which the guest of honour was Queen Elizabeth, the Queen Mother. Her Majesty sat just to the left, behind the chairman on a stage. Naturally, and correctly according to protocol, at the beginning of his speech he turned 90 degrees away from his audience and opened with the words, 'Your Majesty . . .'. Quite rightly, he then established eye contact with the royal personage. Unfortunately, perhaps mesmerized by the lady's legendary charm, he then never took his eyes from hers. Instead, he continued his speech, turned away from the rest of his audience, his eyes boring into the famous azure orbs. At first, Her Majesty politely met his gaze. Then, after a few minutes, she dropped her eyes. He did not take the gentle hint, but went on talking only to her as 2000 people looked on in bemused fascination. Because the executive had, misguidedly, chosen to memorize his talk, he had no need to refer to notes. Therefore, he droned on unabated, his entire being seemingly lost in the depths of that pair of royal blue eyes. Unprecedentedly, but understandably, the Queen Mother began to fidget. She reached down for her bag, she toyed with its clasp, she rummaged through the contents, she even wiped her nose—anything to break the steely beam of exclusive and unwanted attention aimed at her by this apparent maniac.

Nothing worked.

Finally, inexorably, the recitation drew to its conclusion. By this time the audience had, as one, directed its sympathy to the Queen Mother's obvious discomfiture. As the last hollow phrase tripped from the poor man's lips, 2000 people spontaneously burst into wild applause. The noise seemed to rouse the speaker from his royal reverie. Fortunately, he never realized at whom the rapturous response was really directed.

A bad case of royal fever apart, there were other reasons for this speaker's aberrant behaviour. Most important of all, he forgot the sense of what he was doing and saying. Had he remembered those vital factors, he would have turned from the Queen Mother after a second or two's respectful glance and continued as he should have done, directing his attention to the audience. Had he remembered to vary his tone of voice to emphasize word meanings, to use his body naturally to help carry his message along (as much as 90 per cent of meaning is conveyed and comprehended via body language rather than words), these disciplines would have put him back on the right path after any initial royal bewitchment.

Naturally, a bad case of nerves played a major part in that particular royal fiasco. To avoid similar, if less august, mishaps in your own career, it is imperative to relax when giving any presentation. But be careful not to overdo it. Too languid a presentation is not only off-putting, it can also backfire. You need that bit of adrenaline so that your performance has sparkle that will give it life, and to cope with anything that might go wrong.

And things will go wrong. They always do, particularly when you are obliged to rely on electronic equipment. That is why, if at all possible, it is best to have a dry run of your presentation, with a full complement of the equipment you will require, in the venue for which your talk is planned. Ideally, this would take place about an hour or so before you are on the spot. That should give you ample time to acquaint yourself with any necessary amplification equipment, projectors, slide carousels (which you will have loaded and checked yourself) and video machines. If anything is not working properly, and cannot be corrected or replaced to your satisfaction before the presentation, scrap the faulty equipment and improvise a low-tech replacement. After all, if you are only counting on slides and other visual aids for emphasis rather than content, they are not essential.

If, despite your painstaking efforts and safeguards, something still does go wrong, all is not lost. Turn the mishap to your benefit. Even a hostile audience can suddenly turn sympathetic if they see you as a victim of malevolent technology. Again, empathy—this time applied in your direction—can be your salvation. But to win over your audience by being the victim of adversity, you must acquit yourself well despite the calamity. If your sound system goes dead, make a heroic effort to be heard and—just as important—let your audience *know* that you are gallantly doing so on their behalf. If your visual aids let you down, make light of the situation and vividly describe what the audience *would have been seeing* were it not for the miracle of modern technology.

THE EMPLOYEE FORUM

On the subject of hostile audiences, probably the most difficult group of any to address is a roomful of employees gathered specifically to air their questions—and vent their spleens before middle and senior management. It is invariably a volatile situation.

Even the best-managed companies are hotbeds of frustration and misunderstanding. The employee forum can be an effective safety valve for these emotions, but only if correctly handled and staged.

At its most basic, an employee forum consists of every worker in a given location gathered together in as large a room as appropriate to face either an individual senior manager or a panel of the management team. Generally, chairs are arrayed in conventional auditorium style and the speakers are elevated on a podium to allow for adequate sight-lines. This format is a recipe for disaster. What tends to happen is that the senior person will speak for anything up to an hour or so and then open the meeting to questions from the audience. In a large company, stooges from the employee relations department will be lingering on the sidelines with hand microphones that will be shoved beneath the nose of any employee with the temerity to ask a question or raise an issue.

Using your empathetical skills, you can probably guess the usual scenario. The manager finishes his speech, asks for questions, and then silence reigns. Occasionally, there will be a planted question to help break the silence. If done subtly, this is not a bad idea. Unfortunately, however, the fixed nature of the question, and the unlikely identity of the cohort who asks that question, inadvertently reveals the ruse to all.

If there is no planted question, then gradually the frustration will build on both sides. The audience—which in fact will have any number of burning questions they are too frightened to ask—begins to grow bitter with the humiliation of their position. Management, nervous that an awkward situation might be brewing, begins to sweat visibly. Moves are made to bring the meeting to a close, with joking reference to everything being so perfectly understood and everyone being so well informed and happy that no questions arise. Then the dam breaks as several people jump to their feet at once—their frustration transformed to reckless belligerence. To management's chagrin, these hostile questioners are often not the usual troublemakers but those who are normally quiet and compliant. By the time the chairman awkwardly announces time for only one more question, bad feelings are universal. What might well have been a genuine attempt to improve employee communications has actually made matters worse.

What is the alternative? Stage employee forums, by all means, but empathize in the way that you plan them. When are people most likely to be responsive and encouraged to put forward ideas themselves? When they are relaxed. Therefore, split your workforce into smaller groups and plan informal discussion sessions among them and senior management. Ideally, hold these meetings over lunch, or at least over tea, coffee and biscuits. Seat people comfortably around a table, giving them enough space to arrange themselves and their refreshments.

This is not as simplistic as it sounds. In one company the chairman himself initiated a series of employee discussions along these lines. Unfortunately, the stage managing of the event was not up to his good intentions. Coffee, tea and biscuits were served, as they should be. However, everyone was expected to be seated in an open circle of chairs. Where do you put your cup? How do you balance your chocolate bourbon before so exalted a personage? Such are not the thoughts that should preoccupy a file clerk when he or she is supposed to be putting personal views across to the man who runs the company.

Purely practical considerations aside, the presence of a table would have been of psychological benefit as well. Its wooden solidity would have provided a degree of defensive space, behind which participants are much more likely to feel secure enough to speak their minds without feeling threatened.

As for the content of an employee forum, try to avoid a round-robin introduction session in which everyone is asked to give their name and describe what they do. Most of the participants will be so nervously and hurriedly formulating their own introductions in their minds that they will hear nothing of what their colleagues have to say. Instead, equip everyone with place cards that have names and job titles on them in type clearly legible from across the room. Then, begin with a presentation, by all means, but do it in the form of a discussion, and welcome interruptions during the course of the presentation so that the meeting—from the beginning—is seen as a session of give-and-take.

When handled in this way, the employee forum becomes a valuable communications tool for all concerned. The workers are given a better understanding of the business that pays their salaries, and management is much better placed to spot any problems that might be developing or to benefit from shopfloor ideas and initiatives. Most important of all, such meetings, when held with all employees at least once a quarter, foster a genuine and enduring sense of team involvement.

THE PRESS RELEASE

The press release is a highly specialized form of communication. In most large companies, it is originated by the public relations department. Smaller businesses tend to use outside consultancies for this purpose. Less often, senior management might have a go themselves. In all cases, a press release is usually among the most closely scrutinized, widely circulated, frequently altered and least understood means of business communications.

The reason behind this misunderstanding is simple. Effective communication is founded on the principle of knowing your audience. Few business executives know the journalists to whom their press releases are directed. Because they understand neither the reporter's needs nor requirements, the contents of their press releases are usually well wide of the mark.

Though the journalist's role will be examined in more detail in a later chapter, it is worth pointing out at this stage that a well-written press release is a useful tool for a reporter. It tells him or her that something of potential interest is happening in your company. It piques a reporter's curiosity. It gives story ideas—about your company, its products, its technology or your industry in general. It even has direct quotes from the relevant people in your organization. For a lazy journalist, a good release could be a story in itself, with little or no editing required, and giving the illusion—appreciated by less than diligent reporters—that the journalist has actually done some research.

However, all of this relies on the quality of the document. Because journalists might be on the receiving end of dozens of such releases in a day, they need to be able to scan them at a glance and get their full meanings in no more than a minute. For that reason, an effective press release must tell the gist of its story in its headline and first sentence. Anything that follows should merely be an expansion of the basic nugget of information that prompted the writing of the release in the first place.

The actual style of the release is important as well, and should vary according to the topic. You would hardly expect to couch a press notice about a revolutionary new super enzyme plus biodegradable soap powder in the same language used to announce somewhat less-than-remarkable third quarter results. Yet this is often the case with press releases. Nothing is quite so certain to end up in a reporter's waste bin as a release beginning with words along these lines:

NEWS FROM SAFE SUDS

For immediate release:

Safe Suds is a small manufacturer of biodegradable washing powders that was founded 15 years ago in response to a growing awareness of the impact that everyday household washing was having on the environment.

Today, Safe Suds announced that it has formulated a new biological product, AQUA, that not only cleans clothes . . .

A diligent reporter, in the right mood, might just be able to pick up an interesting story idea from that release, but it would involve some work.

Instead, with the same amount of effort expended, the same news about the same product could be announced in a much more effective way:

> **HUNGRY MICROBES TURN GREEN**
>
> For immediate release:
>
> Safe Suds, a pioneer in environment-friendly laundry products, has launched AQUA, a powder that puts a water-treatment plant in every washing machine. Using the most advanced biotechnology, AQUA not only . . .

Any details about the history of the company should be relegated to a 'Note to Editors' section at the end of the release.

Reporters understandably appreciate short, lively releases that tell them the story at a glance. Unfortunately, however, organization management seldom does. When, by managers' standards, such a flimsy document crosses their desk for approval, they are often aghast. Surely, the thinking runs, our story merits more coverage than this. And how can you possibly over-simplify the benefits of what we are promoting by reducing them to a mere sentence?

In other words, management's tendency with a press release is towards the expansive and diffusive, at the expense of the brief and incisive. The result, if these tendencies are not overruled by professional expertise, is a press release that is sent out to oblivion, benefiting neither the reporter nor the company that went to the trouble and expense of putting the thing out in the first place. It is the writer's unenviable, often difficult yet essential task to change managers' thinking on this topic. One way of doing that is a test.

Win the concession that, for once, you will put out a short and sweet press release—just to see what sort of pick-up it gets. Then, make it your business that the release is indeed a success. To do that, time your release very carefully indeed. Gauge the competition. Aim for a slack news period. Or, better still, put in the effort of actually issuing the release at a weekend. A release that goes out on a Saturday or, better still, a Sunday reaches journalists when their news cupboards are relatively bare. With a weekend deadline facing them, they are often desperate for a story or at least a filler. Your release could well fit the bill. Then, come Monday morning, you arrive in your manager's office with a sheaf of clippings. Your point has been proven.

THE NEXT STEP

Having developed a confidence in and mastery of the tools traditionally and conventionally at your disposal, you are ready for wider exposure—and not before time.

The world is being rapidly reshaped by a new communications revolution, akin to but much greater in its impact than the printing revolution of the fifteenth century. The newswire networks with their video link-ups mean that an informal telephone chat with an individual journalist can make newspaper headlines around the world.

More dramatic still, with the proliferation of cable and satellite television throughout Western Europe and the United States, there is more and more broadcasting time that simply must be filled. While some of that time will inevitably be devoted to pure entertainment (or impure if the pornographic channels come into their own), much air space will be filled with cheap-to-produce interview programmes. This trend has already had a major impact on local American cable stations. Combine this with an increasingly confrontational news gathering approach on the part of the more established broadcasting companies, and the typical business executive—who five years ago might never have imagined a television appearance—could suddenly be confronted by a video camera lens across the desk.

It will probably happen to you. The next few chapters could help you get through the likelihood of media exposure, with your career not only unscathed but even enhanced.

4
Getting a fair deal from the ace reporter

In which you deal with the unnerving truth that you are never more than a telephone call away from a journalist. In fact, such a call is probably your first exposure to the media. The journalistic voice at the other end of the wire might be friendly or hostile. You cannot always tell. He or she might be genuinely after some information. Or, just as likely, the reporter might already know more than is first apparent—perhaps even more than you do. It takes discipline, skill and patience to deal with a press call and any subsequent face-to-face interviews that might follow on from that first encounter. This chapter should go some way in instilling the awareness needed for success with the press.

In the previous chapter you learnt how best to put together a press release. Even the best-written press release can never tell every aspect of a story. There is always some loose end, some different angle that will be picked up by any half-way perceptive journalist. Therefore, it is best to regard any press release you issue as nothing less than an invitation to further enquiries. After all, that is why you—or your press officer—put a name and telephone number on the document. If such enquiries will not be welcome—and there are times when a full story is one that you would rather not go public—then it is best not to issue a release at all.

Once you do put out a release and consequently establish that you are open to press enquiries, you must knuckle down and determine what those questions might be. Of course, you already did this to some extent when writing the release in the first place. Now you must go further.

One simple technique is to re-evaluate your finished release from an outsider's point of view. At this stage the object of the exercise is not to revise or improve. You have already done that, and by now the release you are looking at should fully satisfy your own critical faculties and no doubt has been scrutinized by most, if not all, of your organization's management team. Therefore, it reflects their comments as well. Instead, this time round, you should be re-examining the press statement to determine precisely what line or lines of thought it will engender in the journalists who receive it.

This of course will vary according to media type. A trade or specialist journalist will have highly specific process or product-related queries. Local press will always want the local impact of any story. (Legend has it that the *Aberdeen Press & Journal* covered the sinking of the *Titanic* with the headline 'Northeast man lost at sea'.)

Ladies and gentlemen of the tabloid persuasion need a sensationalist approach or the story is no story at all. The more thoughtful broadsheets and weekly reviews will, as you would expect, look to the larger picture and want a better understanding of the long-term financial, commercial, scientific or social implications of your news item.

Not surprisingly, after your previous exercises in empathy, the most immediate way to prepare yourself for any barrage of press interest (and that is, after all, why you put out the release in the first place) is to put yourself in the position of each of these journalists and ask the questions yourself. This exercise should, of course, take place soon before the release is put out. First, write each of these questions down at the bottom of your copy of the release. Then answer them as best you can, consulting other, more expert people in your organization if necessary. Put their answers down in writing as well.

Now you are ready. The release goes out, via fax, telex or hard copy. Within an hour your phone rings. You turn from your PC (no doubt knocking over a cup of coffee in the process), grab for a pad and pick up the receiver.

THE INQUISITION BEGINS

It is *the press*.

But of course it isn't. The voice at the other end merely belongs to a single individual who, despite your trepidations, is not the personification of a hydra-headed, hostile and alien force. Yes, the journalist has a degree of power. But so have you. He or she needs to produce a story. That is simply the way a journalist earns a living. You can help. As soon as you determine who is at the other end of your line, your willingness to help should become immediately apparent in your tone. Be friendly. After all, you initiated this exchange by putting out the release in the first place. But be careful as well.

The first thing to do is to make sure you have a pen and paper available. If press queries become a regular part of your job, the best practice is to keep a particular notebook to hand to record all press calls. Then, begin by taking down the reporter's name and affiliation. Repeat the name to make certain you have it right. You will almost certainly be given both Christian and surnames. Even though it might go against your more formal impulses, use the former. Journalists are used to it, and seem to prefer it. It also helps to establish at least a degree of immediate intimacy that could prove useful. In turn, volunteer your own Christian name in the unlikely event that the journalist is not using it already.

Now it is time to find out exactly what the journalist wants. This could well be something simple, like clarification of some figures or merely a request for a particular photograph. More probably, however, the reporter is after an amplification of the story. Because you have done your homework, you might well have a quick and easy answer in your notes at the foot of your copy of the release. Chances are, however, you will not.

Do not be fazed. Ask a few questions of your own. This simultaneously helps to establish a rapport with the journalist and also gives you a better idea of exactly what angle is being examined; that is, what tone a completed story might take. If you do not want to pursue the matter further, there are a number of ways to cut things short without seeming obviously rude or evasive. You might, for instance, say 'You know, that's a good point. I'll have to check on that. What deadline are you working against?' This gives you time to think. It also lets you know if you can get away with merely letting the matter slip. If the deadline is an hour or so away, you can always indicate that there is only one person who can satisfactorily answer that question, and he or she is out at the moment, but you'll do your best. Needless to say, you will not. The journalist knows that. You know that. Nevertheless, honour is served all round. If the journalist's deadline is not immediately looming, simple ignorance is a good—and frequently honest—ploy. Say you do not know the answer but you will do your best, etc. And then move quickly on. Try volunteering a bit of innocuous information on another tangent that might satisfy your questioner. Or, continue your own interrogatory mode and move the discussion on to an aspect of the issue with which you are more comfortable.

Whatever you do, do not let your unwillingness to answer all or part of a question become apparent. This appears unhelpful, which is a rather churlish thing to be after your own press release invited enquiries in the first place. Above all, avoid the most common and most damaging reply of all: 'No comment'.

Nothing is more thoroughly guaranteed to fire the ire and pique the curiosity of a journalist than those two words. The message they convey is unmistakable: you do not want to help because you have something to hide. Moreover, what you have to hide is, from the journalist's point of view, certain to make a satisfyingly juicy story. No self-respecting journalist lets a 'no comment' go by without using all the professional ingenuity and downright deviousness available to unravel the riddle you have unwittingly set.

If simple evasion of a delicate point does not work, try another tactic. For example, if the precise terms of a contract you have announced are the subject of the enquiry, and you would rather not reveal all, retreat into confidentiality. 'I'm sorry, but the agreement itself says those aspects of the contract are confidential, and you understand we all have to abide by that.' The tone of friendly yet firm reason with which you mouth those words is as important as the words themselves.

TELLING THE TRUTH

Another alternative—albeit a riskier one—is to come clean. This is particularly useful if you know the journalist and feel fairly confident of his or her integrity. There are two ways of doing this. The first is known as 'off the record'. This category of disclosure can apply to either a particular remark or an entire conversation. But to be fair to both sides, the flagging of what is off and what is on the record must be fully understood.

When you are speaking off the record an ethical journalist fully understands the rules that govern that particular part of the conversation. The information supplied is for background only to help the journalist understand more fully the context of the larger topic you are discussing. The information might go so far as to contain specific facts or figures that are necessary for full comprehension of the issue. You can even venture your own or your company's opinions, though this should only be done with considerable caution. Whatever you say, however, the rules dictate that your off-the-record comments are not to be quoted directly, paraphrased or their content implied whatsoever in any press report.

A good (again meaning ethical) journalist is inclined to keep to these rules, if only in the certain knowledge that if the rules are broken, you will never speak off the record again.

A less stringent way of getting a delicate issue across is through a 'non-attributable' press briefing. This means that what you say may be quoted, paraphrased or used in any way as long as your identity, and usually that of your organization as well, is completely safeguarded. Since information given on a non-attributable basis can actually form part of a story, in contrast to the results of an off-the-record session, it is generally preferred by journalists to the briefing from which direct quotes and paraphrases are forbidden.

The drawback to this type of briefing becomes apparent only through repetition. The favoured newspaper phrase of 'sources close to the Prime Minister', for instance, has become an almost universally recognized code to mean the Prime Minister's press secretary. In that way, non-attributable press briefings from the Prime Minister's office have come to achieve a semi-official status—which is probably what was intended all along, thereby giving the Prime Minister an unofficial, but nevertheless authoritative, way of putting out information (or misinformation) that might otherwise be considered unacceptably indiscreet coming from so exalted a source.

FACE TO FACE

British Telecom notwithstanding, there are occasions when a telephone call just will not do. Perhaps a journalist wants more than a few questions answered. Or the story being pursued is too complicated to explain over the phone. Or maybe you yourself are of interest and so an interview is proposed. Conversely, the suggestion for a face-to-face encounter might be your own. This could be part of a larger scheme to get to know the journalists who are relevant to your business or a move on your part to generate publicity on your organization's behalf—or, if truth be told, occasionally on your own behalf. What are the ground rules for a face-to-face encounter with a journalist?

There are none. The occasions, the motivations, the topics are all too diverse. There are, however, certain sensible procedures to follow. The first should be all too familiar by now. Be prepared. Not only will thorough preparation boost your confidence, it will also direct your thoughts and so help shape the encounter. If the meeting is at the journalist's suggestion, it is perfectly reasonable to ask what points he or she would like to cover. You will usually get an adequate reply. If no suggestions are forthcoming, or if the journalist merely wants to wing it, acquiesce but work out in your own mind an agenda of topics you want to cover. This is also what you must do if the meeting is at your suggestion.

Next comes the question of venue, which must be considered very carefully. Other people's offices are always fascinating, which is why most journalists would prefer to come to you. Not only will your office say a great deal about you and your organization, it could also provide additional story leads or at least a colourful peg on which to hang the interview with you. A mere walk down the corridor leading to your office could open up dozens of possibilities for a decent journalist: the condition of the place—luxurious or down-at-heel?—the demeanour of your fellow employees, the announcements on the notice board, even the type of soap used in the washroom. Once the journalist is in your office, more clues about you become apparent. Conspiring to add detail to what might otherwise be a fairly dull and straightforward interview are the pictures on your wall, sales charts, profit forecasts and the correspondence—or lack of it—on your desk.

On the positive side, however, is convenience. If you have a great deal of information to impart, and ready reference to charts, tables, plans or photographs would help you get your story across, then by all means schedule the meeting at your office. Better still, though, is a compromise.

If at all possible, book a more neutral site than your own workstation. Prepare your selected conference room with all the material you need and have an assistant at the other end of a phone prepared to fetch more material that might be required subsequently.

Nor should you forget the duties of a host. On arrival, your journalist guest should be met at the door—preferably not by you—and escorted directly to your appointed meeting place. There, refreshments—tea, coffee, biscuits—should be offered. This seems a trivial point, and it is. But even basic hospitality helps to set the sort of non-confrontational tone that will result in a positive press interview.

At this point the question about use of a tape recorder might well be asked. The usual phrasing is: 'You don't mind if I use this, do you?' You might indeed. Some people inexplicably freeze at the sight of any recording device. Nevertheless, learn to live with it. After all, if you find yourself saying something you shouldn't, the journalist is just as likely to pick it up by reading through notes (journalists take very good notes) as by playing back a tape. One tactic, used by former Labour Minister Tony Benn, has a certain appeal. He makes no objection to a journalist taping an interview, provided the journalist has no objection to the Benn tape recorder humming away in electronic two-part harmony.

If, despite your preparation, you hear yourself saying something you shouldn't, all is not lost. Stop immediately, compose your thoughts, then say, 'If you don't mind, I'd like to rephrase that'. An ethical journalist will forget the transgression, even if it is permanently recorded on tape.

Occasionally, and particularly if the meeting is at your instigation, it might be preferable to talk to a journalist not at your office, but in a restaurant, over an ostensibly relaxed lunch. This has both drawbacks and advantages.

For one, by meeting in a public place, you inevitably lose a degree of control. Acquaintances—either yours or the journalist's—might barge in at any moment. You might not particularly want to be seen talking to the reporter. Or, more confidential parts of your meeting, the off-the-record chat, might be overheard. This particular risk should never be underestimated even when the journalist being entertained is a known friend. The scribe at the next table might not be quite so amicable. Former Tory Cabinet Minister Cecil Parkinson learnt this to his cost during a party conference at Bournemouth. Not only were the fairly lavish details of his menu reported (a first course of Mediterranean prawns at £9, followed by noisettes of lamb in a morel cream sauce at £14.50, washed down by aperitifs, a bottle of Chablis and two bottles of Close La Roche 1983 at £35 a go), but also the contents of his conversation, which were said to include disparaging remarks about some of his Cabinet colleagues. All appeared prominently featured in the pages of a tabloid Sunday paper, to the consternation of the Minister and his more ethical media guests.

While acknowledging the risks of such public press encounters, there are, on the other hand, distinct advantages. If you do not know the reporter particularly well, a restaurant opens up great opportunities for small talk to break the ice. It also, in a subtle yet unmistakable way, puts you in the ascendancy. After all, you are the host; the journalist is your guest. This fact is constantly made clear in a number of small but significant ways. The table is booked in your name. You ask if the journalist would like a drink and what his or her preference might be. You might recommend a speciality on the menu. You choose the wine. You summon the waiter. You pay the bill. You do all of this graciously, of course. But you do it. And the journalist is thus ever so slightly beholden to you. If you handle it well, that emotion will be subconscious. If you handle it badly—usually by being ostentatious in your choice of restaurant or overbearing with the waiters or pretentious in your choice of wine—the inequality of your positions will become all too obvious and your printed interview could well reflect the journalist's discomfort and even anger at what might be seen as an insultingly crude attempt at bribery.

Because a lunchtime interview takes on the trappings of a quasi-social occasion, be careful not to forget the real purpose of the meeting. You want to make a favourable impression on the journalist and so be relatively certain of favourable press coverage in return. Therefore, it is important that you remain quietly in control of both yourself and the situation. If your guest drinks, then you should probably do so as well. However, it is wisest to confine yourself to the odd sip of wine and have water on the table for the serious business of quenching thirst. Since you are there to be helpful, make a show of it. Have a pen and paper to hand so that you can make note of any questions or requests that cannot be dealt with immediately.

Despite the atmosphere of *bonhomie* that you have tried to foster, the odd searching or awkward question might still arise during one of these friendly lunchtime interviews. Be ready for that possibility and take advantage of the mood you have worked to establish to deflect those questions as pleasantly as possible, using such phrases as 'I think that's too complicated to go into here and now', or 'We'll get to that, but first I'd like to cover . . .'. That should do the trick. If your guest persists, be firm but still pleasant and simply declare that you are not sufficiently acquainted with the details to talk intelligently on that aspect of the question.

Above all, the thing to remember in any encounter with the press is this: there is no mystique. You are dealing on a one-to-one basis with a fellow human being who has a job to do. There are certain protocols and cautions you must observe, but that is true of any human encounter.

THE UNEXPECTED CALL

It is one thing to receive press enquiries in the wake of a press release. It is quite another to receive them cold. Sometimes, of course, they can be anticipated, for example, if your company has just had a major round of redundancies, or if takeover rumours are rife, or if you have just raised your prices in a particularly sensitive market. In all of those cases, you should expect press calls and prepare accordingly.

That is not to say you should put out a press release. After all, it is not always desirable to draw attention to what your company is doing—or not doing. But if press attention can be reasonably anticipated, go through some of the exercises that a full-scale release would demand.

This time, however, the results of your catechisms need not go into a formal document. Instead, simply put them down in simple cogent form—in outline, perhaps—and keep them by your telephone. If your gut feelings were correct and the situation does elicit press queries, you are ready. But do not appear to be too ready. A journalist calling to follow up a story lead does not want to hear you reading a prepared statement, or reciting a memorized response. That would be dull for both of you and also indicates that the topic is so important—perhaps more important than initially suspected—that you have gone to the trouble to edit the facts. Instead, try to retain an air of spontaneity. Get your points across, but in a lively, conversational tone that fits in with the questions you are receiving. Take your tone from the journalist, but pitch it down a bit. If the journalist is deadly earnest, you should be serious too—but not quite so serious. You do not want things to sound as dire as your questioner seems to think they must be. If the conversation gets off to a joking start, by all means join in, but keep the laughs under control, or you might find yourself accused in print of flippancy.

Before answering any questions, however, ask a few of your own. After all, this is a cold call, one you did not invite. Initially, your only obligation is one of courtesy. Politely find out exactly who it is you are talking to, and precisely what newspaper, magazine, news agency, radio station or television channel the reporter represents. If anything arouses your suspicion about the enquiry, make an excuse—a call on the other line, perhaps—and take the journalist's name and telephone number. This will not only help establish the authenticity of the call, but it will also give you a bit of time to think things through.

Whatever the nature of the press enquiry, try to establish the context in which the information requested will appear. This will set the tone for your own responses. If possible, and occasionally it is, determine where the journalist got the original information that prompted the call to you. At the same time, assess exactly how much the journalist really knows. Nothing is more exasperating than needlessly giving your game away, when all a reporter really wanted was a few simple answers to a few simple questions. Assess any deadline constraints that might get you off the hook.

If the line of questioning does get fairly heavy and a few queries take you by surprise, do not get flustered. After all, this call was unexpected. Using your friendliest, most helpful manner, simply say you do not know the answer, but if the journalist needs a response, you will do your best to get one.

And so you will—if it suits your needs and those of your organization. If not, let it go. The journalist might not particularly like it, but will understand. If not, another story will soon come along as a distraction. News is, by nature, ephemeral. Therefore, time is usually on your side.

5
The voice of reason

In a significant departure, this chapter launches you into the world of show business with your first prolonged exposure to the pioneer of the broadcast media, radio. Radio provides the perfect half-way house between the printed word and the transmitted image: it does not have the cosy intimacy of one-to-one dealing with a reporter from the print media, but neither does it have the aura and glamour of television. Instead, it is an oddly domestic medium which, for the enlightened amateur, should hold few pitfalls.

It is 7.30 am and you are sitting behind the wheel of your car, stuck in your usual spot in the usual commuter traffic jam.

Your car radio is tuned to the customary station and the disembodied voice of the disc jockey is, as usual, nattering on in an up-beat apparently mindless way. You might occasionally wonder how on earth anyone can go on and on for so long without interruption for either breath or thought, but at the same time you find the noise rather soothing, and at least you can relax in the knowledge that you never have to do *that*.

Don't count on it.

Chances are that if you have any dealings with the media at all, sooner or later you will have the opportunity to put your views across on radio. It is an opportunity that, if handled properly, can invariably be turned to your advantage. But first, it is worth while to look at radio with a degree of objectivity.

Historically, the invention of the instruments needed to transmit and receive audible, intelligible sound signals through the ether must rank as a tremendous breakthrough, a great leap from the wire that immediately preceded it. The discoveries, devices and refinements of Hertz, Lodge and Marconi were the foundations on which the modern media culture has been built.

Before the age of radio, the hearth was the focal point of every household. Since the beginning of the twentieth century, that focal point has shifted. First, it was replaced by the wireless, which provided an unprecedented aural link with the outside world. Then, of course, came the visual medium of television.

If today radio has lost its primacy among the electronic media, it has still come a long way from the days when it competed for attention with the shimmer of a coal fire. Thanks to breakthroughs such as increasing the frequency spectrum and the improvements in sound quality and portability of receivers, radio has become a vital contemporary medium, no longer tainted with the 1930s whiff of Ovaltine.

What, then, is the role of today's radio? In the United Kingdom it serves a variety of functions, depending on whether you are listening to the BBC or an independent station.

The BBC, with all the mighty resources of a state corporation, can still afford to fulfil more of radio's traditional function. It informs, enlightens and entertains. It continues to be regarded as a worthy, professional service and acts as an important training ground—and proving ground—for broadcasters of every type. After all, many of today's leading television personalities started on BBC Radio.

For all its surface gloss—and its production values are among the best anywhere—BBC Radio is still very much an institution. A number of its programmes, such as *Desert Island Discs*, *The Archers* and even *A Book at Bedtime*, have become an intrinsic part of the culture.

Commercial radio broadcasting is another communications animal entirely. It was the first of the broadcast media to benefit from a degree of deregulation almost 20 years ago. The result was a proliferation of stations on both local and national levels. These stations are, for the most part, purely commercial. In other words, they exist first and foremost to make money for their owners. To do that, they must fulfil a number of requirements. First, they have to attract advertising. To do that, they must rely on a sufficient—and if at all possible—growing number of listeners of the right sort (meaning those who will buy their advertisers' goods and services). To attract and keep those listeners, they also need a suitable programme schedule. Of course, the cheapest way to fill broadcast time is by playing records. But doing that all the time satisfies neither all potential listeners nor the licensing authorities who want to be convinced that the station—even though commercial—is providing a public service.

For those reasons, commercial radio broadcasts news, interview programmes and talk shows that echo those to be found on BBC stations. As far as you, the potential part-time broadcaster, are concerned, there is a fundamental difference between the two. But that can wait. First, let us examine what happens should you be contacted to put yourself before one of their microphones. Most likely, this summons will take the form of a relatively straightforward telephone invitation to the studio to put forward your organization's views on a particular topic. What do you do?

The studio invitation is a far from intimidating prospect on several counts. First, you can always stall on your response. Ask the voice at the other end of the phone a few questions yourself:

- What topic or issue has prompted the invitation?
- What programme will the interview be on and who will be the presenter?
- Will there be other guests, and if so, who?
- Will there be sequential interviews or a roundtable discussion?

Once you have that information, you can determine whether or not you want to go ahead. If you want to think about it further—which is an admirable idea—simply stall. Then, use that delay to discuss the opportunity with your colleagues and superiors and use them as a sounding board for the issues that might arise (a technique that will be examined in full in a later chapter).

If, after your rounds of consultation you decide to go ahead with the radio session, relax. It will not be nearly as bad as you might fear. There is something oddly cosy and comforting about radio, and these qualities extend to the radio studio as well. Since the audience, by definition, cannot see what is happening during a radio programme, a conspiratorial atmosphere prevails. It is you—meaning everyone on your side of the microphone—against them, the audience. This results in a camaraderie that develops even during the fiercest-sounding discussions.

Why should this be? The surroundings help, of course. Though technically an electronic medium, radio does not feel that way when you are on the air. No doubt there is a range of highly sophisticated equipment in the control room. Nevertheless, all you have before you is some pretty routine hardware, which, after some very basic instructions from the producer or the host, you will forget about within moments. Because no set designer need worry about things looking sufficiently theatrical, furniture tends to be on the comfortably dowdy side. Like as not, tea will be served in copious mugs—usually chipped.

As for your host and any fellow guests, they are relatively at their ease without the constraints of extraordinary make-up or special wardrobe considerations. In fact, the only shock might be the looks of the presenter. It is a never-ending surprise how deceptive a voice can be in conveying an accurate mental image of physical appearance.

As for any specific behaviour you should follow during the studio interview itself, it is best to conform to the television protocols that will be outlined in a chapter to come. Though the two media are themselves very different, the complexities demanded by television will help you sail through the relative simplicities of a radio studio interview or discussion.

That is the warm and cosy studio side of radio. Somewhat more intimidating is that unexpected moment when the telephone rings and a voice at the other end asks if you would be willing to air your views on a particular topic right then and there. Suddenly, your own office loses its quality of a workplace refuge and takes on the air of a potential public inquisition chamber.

At this point, you must think quickly and act fairly quickly. Ask the usual questions and weigh the responses. If possible—and it should be—ask if you can get back to the caller in a few minutes. Use that time to consider the implications of the request. There is usually not a great deal of harm in refusing. The worst that will usually be said, if the topic is controversial, is that you were unavailable for comment. However, to turn down the interview out of hand might be an opportunity wasted. It is your job to weigh the benefits against the risks and act accordingly.

On a purely technical point, it is also wise to establish what format the interview will take. Will it be live, or will it be edited? Surprisingly, perhaps, a live interview is preferable. At least you know that what you say is what the listeners will hear. On tape, your comments can be cut or edited in such a way as to alter their meaning. Your comments might also be inserted into a context that compromises their intent.

If you decide to go ahead, whichever the format, determine as precisely as possible what the questions themselves will be. Most radio interviewers doing telephone spots are reasonable about this. After all, radio—like nature—abhors a vacuum. A prolonged silence following a question in a normal conversation might indicate thought, but in a radio interview it is highly unsettling for the audience, who immediately suspect that something is wrong with their receivers.

Therefore, to avoid any highly awkward pauses, an element of collusion between you and the interviewer in a telephone session is perfectly natural and—for you—eminently useful. The collusion should not, however, work both ways. You collect the questions and indicate those that you either cannot or choose not to answer (being sure to place the latter into the former category as far as the interviewer is concerned). As for the answers to the questions you have coaxed out of the interviewer, keep them to yourself until you are either on the air or on tape.

This is all fairly straightforward. As described, however, it also sounds fairly passive. A much more active role can be taken specifically with the commercial radio stations.

After all, put yourself in the place of their management. They have hours of empty air time to fill. Their job is to fill those time chasms in a way that is simultaneously interesting (to attract the revenue-generating listeners demanded by the revenue-producing advertisers) and cost effective. The definition of cost effective in this instance is cheap. And what can be cheaper than a virtually ready-made slot produced by a cooperative business or organization that wants to make its products or views known to a wider audience?

The simplest way to go about this is a press release sent to the relevant editor, together with an accompanying letter. This should be followed up by a telephone call that offers your services as subject of an interview.

More complicated, but sometimes even more welcome, is what might be termed an audio press release. This takes the form of a brief tape that covers in either interview or direct delivery form the subject matter you want publicized. This could be a new product, a new service, or expansion plans.

There are, however, some caveats.

Programmers are not fools. They know why you are supplying material to them. And they know you know why they are in the market for such tapes. The tacit understanding between the two parties in such transactions must remain just that—tacit. If you become too overt in what you are doing, you appear to be forcing your material down the programmer's throat. Not surprisingly, this is resented. Instead, you should begin by delicately sounding out the possibility of interest in outside material from your organization. Suggest your choice of topic, but confine yourself to one that would interest the listener as well as your boss. Moreover, resist anything contentious that might merit the right of reply.

If, in principle, a tape would be welcome, there are other factors to bear in mind. Too blatant a commercial message also runs the serious risk of alienating the listening audience you are trying to reach. To avoid this, and to help smooth the passage of your audio release through your local radio station, distance yourself from its production. Get a specialist radio production consultant in to help. Ideally, hire a moonlighting producer from the station itself. This might well help smooth your tape's passage past the editor's desk.

Furthermore, once you have put out an audio release, leave it alone. Do not attach conditions to its use. Do not chase up its progress. If you want to know if and when it has been used, and the station does not volunteer the information, hire a monitoring service to check and provide you with a transcript or tape of exactly what was broadcast.

If all went well, you can be fairly certain that the station will welcome further suggestions from you. If not, put it all down to experience and do not pursue the matter. The last thing you want to do is antagonize or embarrass the station.

Of course, you might not get that far. Some radio stations have rules about such things. Or, while they might welcome a suggestion for an interview, they could draw the line at pre-prepared programmes that are meant to be topped and tailed by their own staff.

Can this pro-active approach to radio backfire? There is always that risk, particularly if it is an interview that you push rather than a pre-prepared tape. Some broadcasters resent it when their guests are, in effect, self-invited. Occasionally, this resentment can manifest itself in tricky questioning, hostile fellow guests or downright rudeness.

If that should happen, there are ways to deal with those problems. The techniques involved are identical to those used in similar circumstances on television.

That is your next step. In the past few chapters you have gone from improving your communications skills from their most basic at a one-to-one level to large-scale presentations and a degree of media control. Now you are ready for the big time. The rest of this book will help prepare you to get your messages across—whatever they might be—to more people, more easily and more effectively than you would ever have thought possible.

6
How you fit into the picture

A brief look at television within its historic and social context. What is there about the conveyance of voice and image through electronic means that alters and heightens perceptions of the messages being transmitted? The chapter also takes a look at the television audience, examining their state of mind, their expectations and, just as important, their preoccupations, as they share a room with the most significant communications breakthrough since Guttenberg.

As a living, breathing example of *Homo sapiens sapiens*, you can trace your immediate species' evolutionary history back some 50 000 years. If you care to go back even further to dig up the first, tender, tentative shoots of everyone's primeval family tree, you could legitimately say that mankind, in one half-way recognizable form or another, has been around for about 5 million years. During that span of time, impressive by any human standards, the species has gradually managed to accumulate a good deal of innate knowledge based on generation after generation of transmitted experience. Adding to and enriching that cerebral database is the more mystic and parochial wisdom known as folk memory.

In the course of human history, the earliest recorded attempts at any non-aural form of communication date back a mere 30 000 years or so with antler carvings and cave paintings. Today, these early relics are considered to be mankind's first works of art. But there is a good chance that they were more than that. They almost undoubtedly had, at least to some extent, some practical communications significance. However, exactly what they conveyed—and to whom—will probably always remain a mystery.

Nevertheless, they are highly significant in any look at communications. As the first of their kind, they demonstrate that though you are a member of a species with roots going back 5 million years, your kind has not been communicating with any degree of sophistication for much more than 0.5 per cent of that time span.

The electronic media—radio and television—in turn, have been in practical existence for less than 100 years (less than 50 years in the case of television), forming only a tiny fraction of that infinitesimally brief period during which mankind has been a communicator. It is hardly any wonder, then, that ordinary people are only just beginning to master the communications miracle they have previously been content to leave to the experts since the beginning of the twentieth century.

THE BACKGROUND

As far as television is concerned, one breakthrough occurred in Germany in the mid-1960s. Peter Tidman, then a young public relations staff officer working with the British Army on the Rhine, was assigned to liaise with both the BBC and 2DF (the second German TV programme) Panorama when they embarked on a series of military documentaries. That was when the Army found itself first bitten by the TV bug.

Having gained a useful insight into production techniques, the Army decided to have a go on its own, with a number of pilot schemes. These covered both news events and features, including royal visits, the peacekeeping forces stationed at that time in Cyprus, and NATO exercises. Those items of the widest interest went to news agencies such as Viz-News for worldwide distribution. Before long, the Army found itself actively involved in the youngest branch of show business.

It was highly exciting for all concerned. But it was also somewhat frustrating. Though the technical quality of the material was improving all the time, the same could not be said for the performance level of the officers who provided the interview fodder for the TV segments. Many were not very good. Some were embarrassingly awful. Moreover, and highly disturbing to so hierarchical an organization as the military, the quality of performance seemed to have nothing to do with rank. Major-generals came across as badly as other ranks, and were often even worse. What was more puzzling, there seemed to be no correlation between the off-camera ability to communicate on a face-to-face basis with success on television. Often, just the opposite held true.

Searching for an answer to this conundrum, an initial theory speculated that the almost consistently poor showings on television might be attributed to the officers' basic inexperience of solo interviews of any sort. This came about because regulations of the time stipulated the presence of an Army public relations representative in any meeting with the press. As a result, on television, without a press officer to metaphorically hold their hands, the army personnel felt highly vulnerable. This vulnerability expressed itself in two ways. Either the interviewee spewed forth in an unguarded fashion or he did just the opposite and clammed up in a manner that could be perceived by the viewer only as highly sinister.

As you might expect, neither reaction made for good television. Nor was it good for the Army or the officers involved.

But was the problem merely a question of fundamental unfamiliarity with interviews in general? After playing back the tapes countless times, that theory seemed too pat an answer. Instead, it became increasingly clear that the fault was not really with these Army personnel—often intelligent and highly personable people in real life—who came across as just the opposite when under television scrutiny.

No, the problem was with the medium itself.

Television, it became apparent, demanded communication techniques that differed from—and were in some cases anathema to—the normal give-and-take of a conversation or even a more conventional, non-video interview.

Exactly what these peculiarly televisual techniques might be was to remain a mystery for a bit longer. The Army, worried that it might be seen to be indulging in Big Brother-like media manipulation, decided to back away from the problem. This reticence proved to be temporary.

A few years later, Northern Ireland erupted in its latest—and continuing—round of sectarian violence. The world's media descended on Ulster en masse. Within days, Belfast's Europa Hotel was packed with journalists and happily obliged to turn away reporters by the score. In all, some 200 reporters, together with 40 international television crews, succeeded in turning what had been, 'The Troubles' notwithstanding, a fairly quiet provincial capital into a media circus.

Included in the copious baggage with which this media invasion travelled was a multitude of prejudices and preconceptions about the role of the British Army in Ulster. Even those neutral in their outlook soon became appalled at the unaccustomed and incongruous sight of heavily armed troops on manoeuvres in civilian streets. Whenever these manoeuvres turned into action, the journalists were there, ready to confront the army officers in charge with a barrage of challenging questions.

The reactions of these officers to unwanted, if not entirely unexpected, media attention varied in several ways. Some tried to turn away or hide their faces in a gesture that came across very much like shame. A few thought that a brisk 'no comment' would be a sufficient and rather neatly professional-sounding answer to any awkward questions. Others made valiant but embarrassingly tongue-tied attempts to explain their actions. Still others soon found themselves reluctantly ensnared in on-camera debate. As you might expect, these exchanges were skilfully lobbed by the professional interviewers and awkwardly returned by the Army personnel. There was, however, a common thread to all the officers' performance in the Belfast interviews. The almost consistently poor quality of their media performances reflected badly on themselves and, by implication, on the Army's already controversial role in Ulster.

It quickly became all too apparent that the Army had to prepare its personnel not only for the conflict in the streets, but also for the battle of the airwaves.

The Chief of the Defence Staff at that time, who had been involved in the Rhine Army television exercises, took quick and decisive action. He ordered that every officer going to Northern Ireland first receive television interview training at the Army School of Instructional Technology in Beaconsfield. That was a start. But what sort of training should the officers receive?

Although television training did exist at that time, it was merely based on the principles of acclimatization or familiarization. Developed, for the most part, by television producers, directors and presenters to supplement their already considerable incomes, such training was probably better than nothing, but only marginally. On the positive side, it did instil a degree of confidence in the officers by getting them used to the camera and the complexities of a television studio. But that was as far as it went. It gave the military personnel no consistent method on which they could rely to remain in control of the on-camera situation.

As for the success rate of the training, who could say? Before the Ulster exercise, such training was largely confined to civilians. At that time, in the relatively early days of television, 1000 civilians could go through such courses and perhaps only half a dozen or so would subsequently ever appear on television at all. With such a small trial sample, it was virtually impossible to assess the value of such courses and even more difficult to modulate the instruction scientifically in order to improve its effectiveness.

Visits to the recognized professional and academic institutes of the period—the BBC, BIM, the IOD, the CBI and the Thomson Television College—were not much more enlightening. Though you could learn how to be a producer, director or floor manager, lighting technician, camera operator or graphics technician, no one was prepared to teach you how to manage or even cope with an interview.

If things in Ulster were not to go from bad to worse, the Army had no choice, then, but to devise a course from scratch. The work developed painfully slowly. Officers, in groups of six or so at a time, were subjected to a barrage of the types of questions they could expect from television reporters on the streets of Belfast:

> 'How does it feel to fire a rubber bullet at a boy of 12?'
>
> 'What would you do if the army marched into *your* home town and started exploding tear gas grenades in the High Street?'
>
> 'In a nation whose Parliament has abolished capital punishment as uncivilized and inhumane, how do you reconcile the use of live, potentially fatal ammunition on a civilian population?'
>
> 'Does your conscience let you sleep at night?'

The theory was that if they could answer these difficult, openly hostile and highly emotive questions in a practice session before camera, they would at least have something to fall back on when confronted with similar queries in real life. In all, some 1000 officers were given this form of preparation by Peter Tidman before they left for Ulster.

After exhaustive review of hundreds of hours of practice tapes, it was found that some of the officers acquitted themselves very well. Yet through no immediately apparent fault of their own, others clearly needed help. (Later, precisely the same situation was found to exist among executives in industry.) But why? Exactly what set the few apart from the multitude? At first, there did not seem to be any answer to that all-important question. But, as the situation in Ulster became ever more incendiary, it was imperative to find one.

The first step in what was to prove to be a lengthy process was to isolate the few good interviews. These were played over and over again. They were transcribed and the texts subjected to intense scrutiny. Slowly—even agonizingly, at first—a pattern gradually emerged.

Either through instinct or intuition, each of the few officers who performed well in his television interview training followed—probably unconsciously—the same simple practices. With observation, it became obvious that these practices were, in fact, inviolate and absolute rules. If you knew them, either innately or though instruction, and then followed them implicitly, you could cope. If you did not, you could not.

So much for the thesis.

Then, having isolated these rules, the next step was to prove the new theory true. This was done by teaching the rules to a sample of officers who had already undergone initial training with the aforementioned, almost universally unsatisfactory, results. The findings of the experiment were at once startling and highly encouraging. Those few officers who had previously been good on television were suddenly tremendously good. The vast majority, whose performance had ranged between appalling and merely indifferent, were suddenly effective on screen.

Their success soon proved to be more than merely clinical. In the field, while giving actual interviews, the corps who had received training in the newly perceived rules of broadcasting were a revelation. The new technique was apparently a success.

To confirm this happy suspicion, and to expedite the training of even more officers, the new course took to the road. (Although it continued at Beaconsfield, as well. There, it was put into service to train senior officers of all services. The Royal Navy, in particular, benefited from the experience since the Cod War with Iceland was in full swing at the time.)

By taking the new television training course to the Rhine Army and to mainland British postings, 1000 officers per year were able to benefit. The practical value of increased television competence across the ranks was almost immediately apparent. A positive side effect of spreading the knowledge was academic. With a greater volume of trained participants available, further research could be done into the critical question of why broadcasting differs from other forms of communication and exactly how to compensate for these differences.

TELEVISION: THE PROTOCOLS AND THE POWER

It is no coincidence that the first step in any contemporary revolution, whether violent or peaceful, is the seizure of the capital city's central broadcasting facilities. In the past few years, events in Prague, Manila, Bucharest, Panama City, Monrovia, Moscow and Addis Ababa are among the latest political upheavals to support that fundamental strategy of modern urban upheaval. Why?

The answer is simple. To control broadcast media is to have a headstart on controlling the information, the ideas and the emotions of the widest possible section of the populace. It does not always work, of course. Bad broadcasting—of the sort that the Ceaucescu regime used in the subjugation of Romania, for example—simply backfires. At first, it is either ridiculed or ignored. Ultimately it only brings the broadcasting powers into disrepute.

But television, as it has evolved in the Western style democracies, hardly falls into the same totalitarian category. Though the relative quality of individual programmes or even entire networks might be open to debate, the potency of the medium is unquestioned. After all, television advertising revenues in the United Kingdom alone account for thousands of millions of pounds sterling every year. Hard-headed, commercially astute advertisers would not have dreamt of committing such a sum if there had been any doubt in their minds about television's power to persuade.

It is agreed, then, that the potency of television as we know it is beyond dispute. But that still leaves a couple of vital questions unanswered. What *is* there about the moving images depicted on a cathode tube that makes them so important? And how do they differ, if at all, from the reality they are supposed to represent?

Starting with the obvious, the size of a television audience can be nothing short of staggering. When the Prince of Wales married Lady Diana Spencer in 1981, an estimated 1000 million people around the world were witness to the royal nuptials. On a more dramatic, though very different occasion, most of the world was united in its rapt attention to the prolonged television coverage of the war in the Middle East.

As far as impact on one particular company and one particular industry is concerned, we need look back no more than a couple of years to the aftermath of the *Exxon Valdez* disaster in Alaska's Prince William Sound. Millions who had never even heard of the place before were transformed, by television, into instant experts in the ecosystems of that remote corner of North America. As a result, and almost overnight in the United States, a new verb entered the national vocabulary: to Exxon, meaning to spill, to make an embarrassing mess, as in 'I was changing the oil in my car and I just Exxoned all over the drive'.

Who are these people who comprise the highly susceptible viewing public? They are made up of every age, race and ethnic group. They include the richest and grandest in the land, and the destitute as well. How on earth is it possible to communicate with so universal an audience and still retain any sense of meaning and identity yourself? The apparent contradiction should be glaring by now. After all, in earlier chapters you learnt that one of the essentials of effective communication is a thorough knowledge of your audience. Yet knowledge of so amorphous a group of people as television viewers must surely be well beyond the scope of normal human comprehension.

Or is it?

When a positive, all-encompassing definition proves to be beyond your ken, often a negative one will do just as well. With that in mind, try imagining yourself in a television studio. You are being interviewed. To whom do you address yourself? Who are your audience? It is difficult to say. So try defining your audience not as what they are, but in the negative, instead.

Collectively, a television audience is nothing like your colleagues at work, who understand your business and the jargon it has evolved. They know little and care less about the problems of your business. The winks, nods and catchphrases you use so effectively in communicating with your colleagues are totally lost on the great British public sprawled before their flickering sets.

Nor does a television audience in any way resemble your friends or family. After all, *they* like you. *They* are kind to you. You can count on *them* to listen sympathetically no matter what you have to say. A television audience, on the other hand, does not know you. What is more, though professional pollsters might classify them as television viewers, that is not all they are doing. They are also talking among themselves, reading, writing, using the telephone, feeding the cat, drying their hair or any permutation among these and countless other activities.

They most certainly do not love you. What is worse, they probably do not even hate you, either. Instead, they are totally indifferent to you, your presence on their television screens and to anything you might be saying.

Nor can you rely on the dignity of your professional standing to protect you. You might well emanate the aura of legitimate authority at work, but your television audience are not at work—at least not at your place of work. They are, for the most part, at home. And at home, the dignities of office are left on the coat rack in the hall. Even corporate chairpersons or chief executives, Cabinet Ministers and Members of Parliament become simply ordinary people when relaxing at home. So why should you, appearing on television in someone's sitting room, be accorded any more respect than them?

And if, by some remote chance, this relaxed, if not actually comatose, audience is tempted to turn from whatever it is they are really doing to glance momentarily at the television screen, what do they see? Nine times out of ten you will be framed by what is known in the trade as 'number one shot'. This directorial stand-by is precisely as imaginative and creative as it sounds, consisting of a head-and-shoulders image cut off at mid chest and surrounded by an invariably neutral background. The rest of you, invisible to the audience, might just as well not be there. What makes the shot even worse than it might initially seem is the complete lack of visual reference points. Without these, there is no way to discern anything else about you. Even the size of your head compared with anyone else's becomes impossible to determine, since the zoom lens enables the director to make everyone appear to the same proportions regardless of any real-life variations. It is hardly any wonder that, when encountering television personalities on the street or at parties, you are usually surprised by either their stature or lack of it.

But let us return to the studio, that strange place where diverse individuals are homogeneously packaged for domestic consumption. The atmosphere in which you find yourself is hyperactive, while you are probably feeling below your best and possibly even downright apprehensive. The bustle about you is disconcerting and somewhat mysterious. The lighting is harsh.

You have been waiting for what seems like hours for your turn to be on, and you notice the programmers have brought on a protagonist who, for the sake of editorial 'balance', is probably going to try to tear you apart.

What do you do?

You either wake up in a sweat from this particularly nasty nightmare. Or you turn to the next chapter. Quickly.

7
Television: playing by the rules

In which the complexities of success on television are narrowed down to three easy-to-follow principles. Each of these is a highly useful communications tool in itself. Put together, these three principles will go a long way in guaranteeing that even a television novice can put on a credible performance in the most potentially awkward of video interviews.

An exhaustive list of do's and don'ts is the last thing you want or need when you are about to undergo the ordeal of a television interview. Fortunately, the basic rules that will take you through the experience triumphantly (or, at worst, adequately) can be narrowed down to just three simple elements.

Before tackling those, however, it is worth putting your mind back to the essence of communication as discussed in Chapter 1. Communication is the business of getting a message from your mind into the mind of another individual or group of people. In normal circumstances, you will seldom try to communicate with more than a roomful of people at any one time. On television, the same process is at work, but you are aiming to get your message across to millions of minds simultaneously. The prospect is naturally a daunting one.

Yet intimidating though television might be, it does have one highly distinct advantage over other forms of communication. Moreover, you can put this advantage to work for you. Simply think back to one of the more persistent clichés you were taught at school:

One picture is worth 10 000 words.

What is television but a series of very quickly moving pictures? If each of those split-second images is worth 10 000 words, calculate the effective amount of verbiage that a mere minute or two of television time puts at your disposal.

It is up to you not to waste that wealth of opportunity. Waste it you will not, so long as you use *each* of the three elements of effective communication:

- You have to attract attention.
- You have to be interesting and so involve the minds of your audience.
- You have to leave a message.

If you fail to attract attention, then your audience simply is not listening. If you are not sufficiently interesting, their attention will wander. If you do not leave a memorable message, there was not much point in bothering to communicate in the first place.

It is well worth looking at each of these rules in greater detail.

ATTRACTING ATTENTION

If good television broadcasters could be said to have a single trade secret, this would be it. Yet their fundamental technique in attracting audience attention is breathtaking in its simplicity. They merely eliminate from at least a segment of their consciousness all the panoply of studio technology that surrounds them. They reduce communication to its most basic one-to-one form. In short, they rely on the second person pronoun to address their viewers as individuals. They use, as much as they can—and even more often than you would believe possible—the one word that everyone most prefers to hear spoken by another person:

YOU

Why should this simple word have such power? Why is it that if you were to shout this word in a crowded street, everyone in sight would turn around? Because whenever you hear the word 'you', no matter who you are or where you are, your mind automatically and instantaneously translates it into the most potent word of all in your personal lexicon:

ME

It works every time, in every language, in every culture. There are, however, subtleties in some languages with differing degrees of familiarity and politesse. In French, for example, there is the 'tu' and 'vous' alternatives. Similarly, German has 'du' and 'Sie'. Classical Arabic even goes so far as to have a different second person pronoun for varying ages and subtle gradations of rank. Nevertheless, with some forethought, an accommodation can be reached in every tongue.

No matter what the tongue, there are any number of variations that can be used to ensure variety in speech. These range from 'all of you' to 'none of you' and all points in between. 'Few of you', 'many of you', 'millions of you', 'one or two of you', 'some of you', 'lots of you'; the list could go on and on. With effective communicators, it does.

Not only does the use of the second person pronoun attract the viewer's attention, it also has the almost magical property of protecting the individual who utters it. For example, imagine that you are the Chairman of British Rail and you have just been put on the spot in a live television broadcast with a searching question about improvements to safety in the aftermath of the Clapham Junction disaster. You can say 'I did this' or 'I didn't do that' but no matter what you say using the first person singular, you are indelibly linked in the viewer's mind with the disaster and whatever degree of carelessness or oversight might have caused it. On the other hand, by responding to questions in the second person, you effectively distance yourself from the problem, and put your audience there instead: 'When you are running British Rail, safety is your uppermost consideration at all times . . .', and so forth. At that point, it is not the Chairman of British Rail who is in the awkward spot, but the viewer. And that viewer, finding himself or herself in the Chairman's hand-made brogues, suddenly and inevitably is obliged to see things from that distinguished personage's point of view. In other words, by resorting to the second person pronoun, the Chairman has managed to harness not only viewer sympathy, but viewer empathy as well.

That is perfect communication. The listener, at least for the moment, becomes one with the speaker.

But the spell can be broken all too easily. Slip an 'I' into your television broadcasting and you suddenly sound pedantic, overbearing and egocentric.

What about 'we'? On the face of it, use of the first person plural might sound appealingly modest and team-spirited. Unfortunately, on television, this is not the case. At best, 'we' comes across as a guilty retreat into group anonymity. At worst, it becomes derisory in its ambiguity. Margaret Thatcher unwittingly provided the perfect first person plural howler when she proudly announced at the door of 10 Downing Street 'We have become a grandmother'. Some pundits mark that awkward comment, that unfortunate, entirely uncharacteristic excursion into collective responsibility, as the beginning of the end of her tenure at Number 10.

As far as television is concerned, 'we' is no one at all.

Neither is 'one' (another pronoun that tends to become part of the excess baggage of ministerial responsibility). Traditionally associated with royalty, the aristocracy and those who would aspire to such dizzy social heights, 'one' is both remote and off-putting. Even the Queen and her family have, for the most part, dropped it from their public vocabulary.

The Princess Royal provides a perfect illustration. Earlier in her public career, as Princess Anne, she used the 'one' form almost exclusively in her television appearances. During that period she was unpopular with both the general public and the media, despite her devotion to and hard work for a number of worthy charitable causes. In more recent years, however, the Queen's daughter has approached her television appearances in a decidedly less formal way. She now uses the second person pronoun in its many forms. According to popularity polls, she has become among the most highly regarded members of the Royal Family. Of course, her almost simultaneous shift in popularity *could* be a coincidence. But it probably is not.

Nevertheless, a few people seem to cling to the use of 'one' as an integral part of their social and intellectual standing. In preparation for the publicity surrounding a planned population census a few years back, the Director General and the statisticians at the Census Office received television interview training. One of them expressed his indignation at the banning of the word 'one'. 'When one's family are all graduates, one naturally uses the "one" in everyday speech. One wouldn't dream of uttering anything so direct as a common "you".'

Fortunately—and unexpectedly—this was a civil servant with a mischievous sense of humour. When actually appearing in quite a tricky television interview, his performance was word perfect, and included not a single impersonal pronoun that might have alienated his audience.

Even if you are not given to such one-upmanship, there are other language pitfalls to avoid. The use of abstract or collective nouns can be particularly offputting. No one sees himself or herself as an end-user, a consumer, a member of the general public, a reader, a listener, a viewer. And who, in his or her right mind, would choose to identify with a 'throughput'? Yet BAA (formerly British Airports Authority) persists in referring to—and worse still directly addressing—people in this most offputting of manners.

One of the most misleading collective nouns used by careless broadcasters is 'housewives'. 'When the housewife goes shopping, she should keep her eyes open for the value offered by the shop's own brands,' the sloppy presenter might say. This is a mistake. Women do not think of themselves as housewives. They do not even think of themselves as women any more. Like everyone else, they define themselves by their livelihoods. Therefore, the proponent for in-house labels should simply say to his or her audience: 'When *you* go shopping *you* should keep *your* eyes open, etc.' By using the all-embracing second personal pronoun, you hit every target individually: old age pensioners at the Royal Hospital, children out on errands, the bond salesperson at lunchbreak, the traffic warden on the beat, and even—that vanishing species—the woman with no outside employment who chooses to focus her activities on the domestic front.

When you are careful to address everyone who can hear you on television—and that can mean tens of millions of people—exclusively using the second person pronoun or one of its many variants, you are speaking to everyone as an individual. You are excluding no one, and giving no one the opportunity for self-exclusion. You have grabbed your audience's attention in a way that is foolproof since it simply echoes everyday conversation:

'You've just eaten the last of the cornflakes.'
'You look pale this morning.'

'Will you pick up the drycleaning?'

'You'll have to tell your mother that you can't make it tonight.'

Even the most banal subjects can take on a personal immediacy when couched in the second person format. You do not have to be a gardener to hang on to every word of Percy Thrower's broadcast on growing tomatoes when it is put like this:

'If you are growing tomatoes you want to be watchful at this time of the year. Take a look at your plants. If you see something growing in the junction between the main stem and the main branches then take your thumb and rub it out. If you do this you will reduce the foliage and get better tomatoes.'

Out of 59 words, seven are variants of the second person pronoun and two further second person pronouns go implicitly with the verb forms Thrower uses. As a result, when you hear this spoken, you can distinctly visualize tomato plants before your eyes. You can see the growth he talks about and you can almost feel the cool ooze of liquid from the torn bud as you scrape it off the stalk.

There is an ancillary, but none the less important, advantage that comes with the discipline of confining yourself to use of the second person pronoun. Because you are using a conventional, everyday form of speech, you are much less likely to suffer from the nerves that often breed pomposity in public speakers. By using 'you' and its variants, your television appearance does not come across as an address or a lecture or a delivery or an oration. (One of the reasons for Queen Victoria's legendary dislike of her longest serving Prime Minister, Sir William Gladstone, was that politician's way of speaking to his monarch. 'He addresses me as though I were a public meeting', she complained.)

The second person pronoun ensures that everything you say on television becomes part of a person as well as personable conversation. The fact that it is perceived as such by several million people simultaneously should be incidental to your own performance.

Because you are engaged in a personal conversation, you do not begin an appearance on television with the deadly, but all too usual:

'I have to thank you for the opportunity afforded to me to address you this evening.'

Or the cringing, but now probably archaic:

'Thank you for letting me into your living-rooms.'

There is not even any need to say 'Good morning' or 'Good evening'. After all, you are already there, as far as the audience is concerned and if everyone observed that nicety, television would be even more boring and repetitive than it already is.

Instead, get to your point. Immediately, if possible or with a preface such as:

'You probably know that . . .'

This simultaneously flatters your listeners by assuming their implicit knowledge of your subject while spelling out exactly what your subject will be.

You now have your audience's attention. Your next objective is to keep it.

RETAINING ATTENTION

To keep your audience's attention, you must know who they are. Their age range spans infancy to senility. In terms of class, you could encompass everyone from the homeless in a temporary shelter to the denizens of the Palace itself. Educational attainment stretches from functional illiteracy to doctoral theses. So whom are you aiming for when you appear on television?

Think of the legendary Clapham omnibus. For some reason, this public conveyance has taken on an all-important position in the theory of British mass communications. Reach one of its passengers, conventional wisdom has it, and you reach the nation. This is probably no longer true. Gentrified Clapham, with its wine bars and festoon blinds, is rather less of a social barometer than it used to be. However, if your communications loyalties remain with the Clapham omnibus, aim not for one of its passengers, but for the driver instead. And while you are at it, consider the driver's family as well: the children, the parents, the in-laws, the neighbours. Every broadcast syllable you utter must be readily and easily understood by all of them. If your words are not instantly comprehensible to them, they will dismiss you as a boring old fool and either ignore you or switch off entirely. If you make the even worse mistake of talking down to them, of being seen to patronize them, they will hate you forever.

As you already know, the way to attract your audience's attention is to begin on a conversational note, using the second personal pronoun and its variations *ad nauseam*. The way to keep audience attention is to continue in this vein, and confine your conversation to a style and content that will keep them listening. This is particularly important if your topic is intrinsically technical, scientific or otherwise on the dry side.

An American television rule of thumb bears repeating. Never say anything in a way that could not be readily understood by a slightly backward child of 12. This is not to malign such a child. Far from it. In fact, persuading children—at least initially—is probably the most successful way of ultimately getting a message through to their parents. Advertisers were among the first to grasp this important notion. Television commercials for such products as breakfast cereals, theme parks and holiday camps are all overtly aimed at children. This is not because children themselves have that much significant purchasing power, but because they can persuade their parents about which of these purchases to make. You have only to watch a child in a supermarket to see how important is the offspring's contribution to the total contents of the shopping basket.

On a more serious level, consider the way in which the ecological movement has percolated upward. The BBC's *Blue Peter* programme, for example, was in the vanguard of the recycling movement and an early critic of the fur trade. By converting juvenile viewers to these causes, the programme's producers went a long way in raising the national consciousness about these issues. It is difficult to toss a glass bottle in the dust bin when your child can confidently stand by and recite how much energy would be needed to duplicate that discarded receptacle. Similarly, how many children today would permit their mothers to attend a school event swathed in furs—even if they were minks specifically bred and reared solely for their glossy pelts? Logic does not enter into it. The highly persuasive and all-pervasive power of children does.

Because you must aim for that important 12-year-old, does that suggest you condescend to your audience? It need not and you should not. Instead, just pay close attention to the way you are using the language. Jargon and acronyms, for instance, are instant death to comprehension. When you think about it, it is hardly surprising. Such forms of speech are, after all, part of the trade language of experts; the linguistic shorthand shared by a self-selected few. Why should you expect anyone outside your company or industry to understand them, let alone a television audience? Yet how often have you heard—if not actually listened to—a nervous expert retreat into the security of shop talk?

Oil executives, for some reason, seem particularly prone to this fault. For example, some years ago in Norwegian waters, the Ekofisk offshore oil production platform suddenly experienced a blowout—an uncontrolled release of oil and gas under very high pressure. It was the first time such an incident had occurred in the North Sea and so it attracted the world's press. Phillips Petroleum, operator of the field, gave a very good press conference under the leadership of its local general manager, who happened to be an American. All went well until a question about the cause of the incident arose. 'Wasn't it true', a journalist asked, 'that the reason for the blowout was a valve that had been put in upside down?' Rather than refuse to speculate, or to admit that was the case, the unfortunate general manager sought to refute not the charge itself, but the direct way in which it was worded. 'No,' he said. 'The valve had not been put in upside down. Technically, it was in "inverted mode".' He made his point. And simultaneously lost his case.

Simple sentence structure also plays an important role in retaining your audience's interest. Always keep to the active voice in your pronouncements; entirely avoid the passive. A maker of agrochemicals might, for instance, say in defence of the company's herbicides:

'You don't want poison ivy in your jam, do you?'

Which is a much more effective way of saying:

'It is imperative that food products in their agricultural stage be free of any potentially hazardous extraneous herbaceous substances.'

Again, just as you attracted audience attention by speaking on a one-to-one basis, use the same technique to retain that attention. That is exactly what you would do in ordinary conversation: enriching your talk by thinking back to your own sensual impressions, giving examples of what *you* have seen and what *you* have done. Provided you consistently apply the first rule of broadcasting—to use the second personal pronoun or its variants at every opportunity—such reminiscences can be little short of gripping.

After all, put yourself in your audience's place (empathy, yet again). It is not every day that you have the opportunity to learn, *first hand*, what it is like to work on an oil production platform, or to juggle the cash flow of a multinational corporation or to put into effect massive changes to the nation's tax structure. All of these activities are normally the preserve of highly trained, highly valued and no doubt highly paid experts. Yet a successful television appearance can convey what it would be like to share in that expertise, if only momentarily. Your audience appreciates that brief excursion from their own relatively mundane lives and so gives you—and your message—the full attention you merit.

The technique for garnishing your appearance with appropriate anecdotes is refreshingly straightforward. Simply introduce an illustrative example by prefacing it with 'For instance . . .'. Every time you feel yourself becoming dull or banal in a television appearance (or, for that matter, in everyday conversation as well) simply interject those two words and your discourse suddenly comes alive again.

LEAVING A MESSAGE

If there is any valid reason for subjecting yourself to ordeal by television camera, leaving a message must be the primary one. Yet it is a highly challenging prospect. It is one thing to attract attention and then keep it for a few minutes. It is quite another accomplishment to use those few minutes to imprint a lasting message on your audience's collective and individual consciousness.

Fortunately, the problem is not a new one. Much the same dilemma faced the founders of the two great Western religions. Consider the difficulty of persuasively conveying the concept of a single, invisible, omnipotent God to a society that grew up on a diversity of icons, both visible and tactile.

Such a difficult idea could only be put across by using the most vivid and stirring images.

Take, for example, the episode of the parting of the Red Sea, from the Bible's Book of Exodus. Even in the days before Cecil B. de Mille that powerful picture was an enduring part of the Western world's consciousness. If you stop to think about it, you might question the details. You could justifiably ask what actually happened to the water molecules to cause the parting. You might wonder what happened to the fish. And, to be absolutely honest, wasn't the freshly exposed sea bed a bit on the muddy side for convenient passage by Israelites loaded down with all the bags and baggage necessary for their arduous journey across the desert?

You might be sceptical. You might not believe any of it. But you cannot forget either the image itself or the idea of divine omnipotence that it conveys.

Not surprisingly, Christianity followed Judaism's lead in relying on highly vivid detail to carry the weight of the heavier truth. In the Gospel according to St Matthew, for instance, Christ's complex divinity is illustrated by another aquatic feat. Having sent his disciples ahead in a boat, he joins them later '. . . in the midst of the sea, tossed with waves . . . walking on the sea'. When Peter wants proof that it is indeed Jesus skimming the briny and not a malign spirit, Christ reaches out his hand and orders his disciple to join him in performing the impossible. This Peter does, walking on the water to Jesus. 'But when he saw the wind boisterous, he was afraid; and beginning to sink, he cried, saying, Lord, save me. And immediately Jesus stretched forth *his* hand, and caught him, and said unto him, O thou of little faith, wherefore didst thou doubt?'

It would be difficult to come up with a more compelling and memorable way of illustrating the power of belief, the torment of doubt and the ultimate redemption of faith.

This is not to say that your broadcasting technique should assume biblical overtones. But there is something more than religion to be learnt from the Western world's most influential volume. If you want to get your message across as effectively as possible, speak in as visual a way as possible. Stanley Hyland, a distinguished producer and a television doyen at the BBC, once put it very well:

'Broadcasting is rather like talking to someone who is blind. It is your job to fill in all the bits and pieces so, with your words, they can actually see a picture. For instance [there is that phrase again], if you were taking a blind man through a rose garden, you might say 'watch the steps and the French doors. You can hear the gravel now as we walk towards the rose arbour and you can feel the rose thorns tugging at your coat. Now you can smell these gorgeous blooms. As we move on you can hear the fountain tinkling away and you can smell smoke from the embers of the bonfire and hear the birds flitting from branch to branch looking for greenfly.'

It is not difficult. In fact, you no doubt use a degree of imagery in your speech at least to some extent already. The trick is in keeping your imagery fresh and not resorting to clichés. After all, a cliché is nothing more than a vibrant image that has been around too long: water under the bridge, light at the end of the tunnel, mending fences, flat earth policy, shooting yourself in the foot, pulling the wool over your eyes, throwing money at a problem, concrete jungles, between the devil and the deep blue sea, biting the bullet, grasping the nettle. Each of these expressions was brilliant when first coined: the lustre has simply worn off with too much handling.

There is another danger associated with clichés, as a chairman of the Institute of Directors (IOD) discovered, to his cost. They trip too lightly from the tongue, not always with your full intent. One noteworthy occasion was during an interview about the quality, training and integrity of directors in British companies. At that time, the then-chairman of House of Fraser had just received less than favourable publicity for accumulating gambling debts of £500 000. Another prominent company director was awaiting extradition to Hong Kong on charges of dubious dealings. When questioned about these less than laudable activities on the part of leading British industrialists, the IOD director's reply was a dismissive: 'That's merely the tip of the iceberg'. What he meant to say, of course, was that every barrel always contains one or two rotten apples.

In general, then, clichés are best avoided. But something happens to a cliché when it has been around for some time. Gradually, a cliché with enough of a past becomes a homily. 'There's no smoke without fire', you might well have heard at your grandmother's knee. It was hardly an original phrase in her grandmother's day, nor is it particularly colourful. It is, however, hoary. Such a venerable phrase, and those like it, impart a timeless truth and respectability to any relevant point you might care to make. But again, homilies, like clichés, should never be used mindlessly, lest they backfire. That can be amusing for your audience, but devastating for you.

Consequently, whenever possible, stick to your own words—despite the fact that it is difficult for most people to come up with original and apposite imagery to enliven a particular discourse. But it is well worth the effort. Newspaper research by Reinsch bears this out.

He prepared three versions of an article urging restrictions on police powers to tap telephones. One-third of the participants in the study received and were asked to read a straightforward editorial. Another third made their way through the same basic editorial enlivened with four similes such as 'a wiretap is like a one-way mirror in your living room', and 'a telephone is like a confessional box'. The rest of the readers surveyed received the basic editorial made more vibrant with four metaphors. (These were identical to the similes, but minus the direct comparison established with the word 'like'.)

The findings were conclusive. The version of the article with similes was significantly more persuasive than the basic literal editorial. The metaphorical version was much more persuasive than the one using similes.

Why should this be? Metaphors communicate by using several mechanisms. They increase the audience's attention, they enhance the apparent competence of the speaker (or writer) and they establish an aesthetically satisfying context. Additionally, and no less importantly, the use of metaphors flatters the audience on the sophistication of their comprehension.

Yet how do you apply the literary standards of the well-written editorial to a few moments' appearance on television? Fortunately, you seldom appear on television without at least some warning. The medium is not nearly as spontaneous as it looks. Therefore, given a bit of time and a modicum of imagination, you have every opportunity to prepare a range of appropriate mind pictures.

ADDING IT UP

For someone who is not a professional presenter, any television appearance is an occasion fraught with peril. So much can go wrong, and in front of so many people. Nevertheless, among all the media, it is the one that can ensure your presence will have a major and positive impact—provided you attract and hold the attention of the audience, and then present your all-important message in as memorable a way as possible.

But there is little point in following these three simple rules of broadcasting if there is any doubt about your overall objective. Exactly what do you want to get across to the viewers?

Answering that all-important question is not as straightforward a process as it might first seem. It requires a good deal of forethought, detailed research and a complete understanding in your own mind of what your television appearance is meant to accomplish. If you do not do this homework, as set out in the following chapter, you would be better off leaving the enormous risks and even greater rewards of television to those who do.

8
Just get to the point!

Stressing the importance of information distillation. Television is all about time, a limited and highly expensive commodity. That is why before any television appearance you must do some preliminary editing of your own. What do your audience already know? What do they need to know? What do they want to know? You cannot answer such awkward questions without first asking them of yourself.

No contemporary Christmas in Britain is complete without the family gathering around the cosy glow of the colour television set in the lounge to watch the Head of State convey her seasonal greetings to the Commonwealth. In this annual media highpoint of the royal year, Her Majesty Queen Elizabeth II, Queen of the United Kingdom of Great Britain and Northern Ireland, Defender of the Faith, etc., can count on at least 10 minutes of television time.

Humbler folk must rely on rather less. In fact, if you were appearing on a network broadcast, you might count yourself lucky to have 15 *seconds* in which to get your message across to several million people.

Contrast this with the time you would normally allocate for full-scale, in-depth interview by a newspaper journalist. During the hour or so devoted to that exercise, you could expect to go over the same ground several times. You could repeat and rephrase any awkward questions and then clarify your responses. At the end of the session, though you could by no means guarantee the quality and tone of any article that comes out of the interview, you would at least be confident that you had communicated your point—in all its complexity—to the reporter and so, you hope, to the newspaper's readers as well.

On television, you can expect no such luxuries. From start to finish, the average interview lasts no more than two and a half minutes. Within that time, the interviewer sets the scene, probably runs some video footage and then brings in a protagonist. That leaves you with no more than a minute of actual speaking time.

What can you say in a minute?

First of all, it might be worth examining what you must *not* say.

Explanations, for one, are out. They simply take too long. This is unfortunate, since explanations—comprehensive, thoughtful, precise, well reasoned and invariably lengthy—are standard behaviour for the business executive. Ask a business man or woman a question, and you will get an oral dissertation in response, beginning with an introduction, moving on to a discussion phase which might incorporate such subheadings as manpower, technology, finances and timetables. Then, of course, there are the options from which to choose and finally the recommendations that lead to a summing up and then to the long-awaited conclusion. In everyday life, there is nothing wrong with this. Indeed, a well thought out explanation is a wonderful thing. Except on television. There, it is death by camera.

As already stated, many television appearances are not more than 15 seconds in length. In that time, talking on even the most basic of topics, you would barely get through the first line or two of your introduction before the interviewer would cut you off. As for any conclusion you might have hoped to get across to the viewers, that opportunity is lost forever. Instead, you have put across the idea that you are a pompous windbag. But that is not all.

When you are invited to appear on television, you automatically represent your business or organization. A policeman who comes across as PC Plod discredits not only himself, but also the constabulary at which he is based and the whole police force in general. He becomes, in effect, the concept of policedom personified. The fact that others in the force might well be bright and intelligent is immaterial to the viewer. The impression made by that unfortunate television appearance is what lasts.

A television appearance is therefore a heavy responsibility to bear. Fortunately, it is not one you have to shoulder alone. Instead, though only one person from a company might actually appear before the cameras, any television interview should be regarded from the start as both a collaborative and a collective effort.

What this combined effort must set out to achieve is a series of concise, memorable and irrefutable statements. Each of these statements must be able to stand alone. And each, when put together with the rest, must form a building block to the greater truth about your business or organization and its operations.

Why the truth?

The moral dimension apart, it is vital to tell the truth on television simply because it is so readily apparent when you do not. No better lie detector has ever been invented. How often have you watched a politician or industrialist respond to a question and heard yourself—almost involuntarily—muttering to the screen: 'He's lying!' Just why lies should be so readily apparent on television is still something of a mystery. Though undoubtedly some people can and do get away with it, most are exposed—or rather, they expose themselves. Through some alchemy, television manages to magnify those slight, almost imperceptible signals we all give off when mouthing an untruth: a slight shift of the eye, a tightening around the lips, a few beads of perspiration glistening in the cleft of the chin, or a barely perceptible quaver of the voice. Every twitch or hesitation, recorded in unforgiving close-up, instantly gives the game away and transmits a record of your dishonesty to millions of homes simultaneously. It is a sobering thought, and one that should steer everyone who appears on television on to the straight and narrow path of candour.

Yet even the truth is, unfairly and paradoxically, no guarantee of credibility or even plausibility on camera. Those qualities can only be relied upon after some fairly exhaustive—and collective—work before the cameras ever start rolling.

Sometimes this work is done in a hurry. Emergencies—those occasions when you are most likely to be called to account in front of the cameras—have the virtue of concentrating the mind wonderfully. But more and more business executives are being invited to give their views on more routine occasions. This is hardly surprising when you take into account the amount of time that is available to be filled with the proliferation of satellite, cable and tape technology—not to mention the arrival of new conventional broadcasting stations in the United Kingdom.

The implications of this media proliferation are obvious. The time is fast approaching—if it is not already here—when anyone in any moderately responsible role in industry, local government, central government, the law, the arts, the professions, the trade unions can expect to be invited to broadcast.

That being the case, it is in the interest of everyone in an organization—and in the interests of the organization itself—to be ever ready for this video inevitability. Such preparation consists of the ability to summarize your organization's point of view on any number of topics or events related to your business: what has gone right, what has gone wrong, what might go wrong, what you want to see happen in the future, what you want to stop happening. In other words, you must embark on a programme of issues management, but the discipline of television requires that you take issues management one step further. This step is known as reductive communication, the reduction of explanations to statements.

GETTING DOWN TO THE GIST

Imagine that your company produces a product that has been accused of being unsafe. You have been invited to give your company's side of the story to the consumer segment of your region's local television news report. Assuming you accept the invitation (whether or not you should will be discussed in a later chapter) what on earth are you going to say?

As you already know, you are *not* going to give an explanation. Instead, you must know in advance what few statements you want to get across in response to—or in spite of—the questions that might be put to you.

The first thing you should do is meet with anyone in your company who has anything valid to say on the subject. Among your subordinates, peers and superiors anticipate what you will be asked. Tear your product to pieces. Show no mercy. (Your interviewer certainly will not.) List everything that could possibly be wrong with the product and, together, come up with suitable replies should those faults be brought up during the course of the interview.

Then go one step further. Talk about the company as a whole. Does it have a history of faulty products? What is the basis of its financing? How are employee relations? Are there any union troubles? Is a takeover bid in the offing? It does not matter that these issues might have no relevance at all to the ostensible topic of the interview.

Now, cast your net wider still. What is the reputation of your industry as a whole? Have there been faulty products produced by other companies? The misfortunes or misdeeds of one operator can and do have a bearing on the reputation of its competitors. Guilt by association may not be fair, but it does make for good television.

If you can come up with some interesting questions about these side issues, you can be sure that your interviewer can as well. Yet again—and not for the last time—you empathetic skills must come into play.

You must also exercise a degree of empathy in your discussions with your colleagues. After all, at least some internal friction is inevitable when discussing such potentially emotive topics. What suits the people from personnel might not suit the production manager. And financial boffins will always see things in a perspective that differs radically from the salesforce's point of view. Nevertheless, this internal strife is an inevitable and worthwhile process.

Since this brainstorming session can be a somewhat emotive ordeal, it is important to have someone outside the discussion take neutral and copious notes of the proceedings. From these notes, and after no doubt lengthy consultations with everyone involved, you can produce an interview model.

In the lead-up to the privatization of the UK water industry, this is just what one of the companies involved decided to do. It was a wise decision. The privatization itself was controversial, and came at a time when the quality and quantity of Britain's water supply was seriously questioned due to several years of drought and several decades of underinvestment. In Cornwall an entire community was apparently suffering the aftereffects of water poisoning. In other locations the water had turned decidedly sinister shades of brown and red. One Essex area even had worms on tap. The media were, as might be expected, on top of the situation. And so, this particularly prescient water company decided to prepare themselves for the day when media attention turned their way, either because of the fairly unpopular issue of privatization itself, or because something awful had happened in their watery bailiwick.

What do you do to prepare yourself for the unthinkable? The answer is obvious. You force yourself to think about it. With prompting, senior executives in the company came up with a suitable interview model, encompassing both the issue of privatization and the more emotive topic of water quality and the environment. The list of issues covers more than 70 topics and is reproduced as it was created, in no particular order:

- What changes will occur on privatization?
- You will have the same people/technologies/procedures. How will you improve your operations?
- How will you inject a new motivation into people?
- Are you looking for high flyers to join you?
- Your government dowry is £150 million and your debts are £400 million. How will you clear those obligations?
- Will you manage your finances better in future?
- Will the same financial managers be in charge?
- Why should they do better this time around?
- Will there be financial training?
- Why are you still discharging aluminium sulphate into your rivers, despite the experience in Cornwall?
- How do you deal with runoff of agrochemicals and pesticides?
- How do you deal with industrial pollution of the water supply?
- What happens to runoff from sludge spread on the fields?
- Why do you allow 40 000 tonnes of sludge a year to be dumped offshore?
- Why have you banned canoeists on your rivers in favour of Yuppie anglers?
- How are you handling discharge from fish hatcheries?
- What are you doing about discoloration of the water supply?
- How are you combating scum, bubbles and worms in the water?
- Is fluoride safe?
- Why have you spent millions on computers but nothing on better service to customers?
- Why are you spending £30 million a year on television commercials?
- Are you co-operating with Friends of the Earth, the Pure Water Society and other groups?

- Is radiation in the water a threat to health?
- Why is the cost of water likely to soar?
- What about the 25 per cent of your customers who already find charges too high?
- Are you contracting out labour?
- What are your managers doing to relate to the local communities?
- What is the policy on water meters?
- How much will they cost?
- How long will they last?
- Why aren't you making the meters yourself?
- What reserves do you have for product liability emergencies?
- Can anthrax infect the water supply?
- Why do we run out of water during the shortest of dry spells?
- What have you got to show for all the money spent since the big drought in 1976?
- If you've spent thousands of millions making reservoirs safer, does that mean they weren't safe before?
- How can you justify pushing up charges just to pay dividends to shareholders?
- What about redundancies to reduce the wage bill and push up profit?
- Why are sewers suddenly collapsing all the time?
- Are there dangerous reptiles alive in the sewers?
- Can they come up through the lavatories?
- What are you doing about the growing rat population in the sewers?
- Does our water supply carry Weil's disease from rat urine?
- Is there a danger of sewer explosions from methane?
- What about hydrogen sulphide?
- What is happening to industrial water rates?
- Are you going to charge for clean water going in and effluent going out?
- Why do you give discounts to well-off people who pay in advance?
- Is the water contaminated with heavy metals from industry?
- What are you doing about lead pipes in old houses?
- Do washing machines have check valves to prevent soiled water getting into the water supply?
- Are we getting lead poisoning in areas where the water is acidic?

- Are manganese levels too high?
- What will happen to all the land you own when you are privatized?
- Are you going to build desalination plants?
- What will they cost?
- Who will pay for them?
- Are you going to diversify?
- Can AIDS from hospitals infect the water supply?
- What are you doing to prevent legionnaires' disease?
- Is there hepatitis B in the water?
- What about botulism?
- Is your water causing a kidney stone epidemic?
- Why is there such a high concentration of *Escherichia coli* bacteria in the shellfish in your area?
- How are you stopping farmers from dumping diesel in the rivers?
- What about silage discharges from farms?
- Are you planning any more dams or reservoirs?
- Are your groundwater sources polluted?
- Do you have enough staff to monitor abstractions?
- Are you going to sell what was public land to developers?
- Are you going to restrict land access to ramblers?
- What is going to happen to your salary costs when you go private?
- Is the government turning a blind eye to water problems by agreeing to accept lower standards from privatized companies?
- What will Brussels say to violation of European standards?
- How are you making managers more commercially aware?

The list can and did go on. Its compilation cleared the mind and got the executives and managers to concentrate objectively on the issues and problems with which they were faced. More important, they were able to see them from the same vantage point enjoyed by those outside the organization.

Nor did the water company managers stop there. They also came up with a useful list of words and phrases that should be avoided in any media response, either because they are jargon, technical shorthand or merely executive speak. In their particular business the list encompassed:

- potable water
- other units
- raw water
- indicators
- new water bodies
- fixed charge basis
- abstraction
- acidification
- alleviation schemes
- bathing use areas
- conjunctive use
- design criteria
- determinations
- discharges
- disposition
- EC designated beaches
- desalination
- deepols
- Dwrpols (pollution of the Welsh river Dee)
- rotacuts
- singular points
- license
- scrutinize and approve
- single points
- statutory objectives
- freedom to discharge
- low flows
- organic
- pathogens
- point sources
- precepts
- riparian owner
- specifiers
- overtopping
- mode of transmission of water
- fixed parameters

- plethora
- tankering
- boilers

That done, the watermen tackled each of the points raised in the brainstorming session, argued them through, and then arrived at agreed and simple statements which responded—or at least seemed to respond—to any question on that particular topic.

Not that it is always easy coming up with the right statements. They have to be simple, personal, informative and honest. If it is tough to arrive at these statements when you and your colleagues are sitting around a table together, think how much more difficult it must be if you try to wing it and come up with the appropriate thing to say during the course of an interview itself, when you are feeling at your most vulnerable, anxious and apprehensive. That is why the distillation process must take place well before the cameras begin to roll.

The experience of a travel industry managing director provides a good illustration. His company specializes in package tours to the Costa Brava. Every year Basque terrorists toss a number of bombs in the main tourist areas to scare off the trade and so pressurize the government. And every year, like clockwork, when this happens the television networks ask the managing director to give his view on this tense situation. What do you say if you are in his shoes? You cannot reply:

'Go to Spain anyway. It's perfectly safe.'

That could expose the company to a lawsuit from anyone who was injured in a bomb attack after following that advice. On the other hand, since your livelihood is at stake, you are hardly going to say to the interviewer and the television audience:

'The political situation in Spain is very tense just now. I recommend you cancel your plans for a holiday there.'

However, with a bit of forethought and much discussion with your colleagues, you will no doubt arrive at a simple, straightforward and positive statement that your audience will find both comprehensive and credible:

'Go on your Spanish holiday, but take the same precautions that you would follow if you had a bomb scare at home.'

Such a model succeeds in pre-empting any surprises that might arise from a hostile interviewer or any other protagonist in the television studio. Forewarned is forearmed. This serves to enhance your confidence before the camera. It helps to get you in your stride and allows you to take control of the interview, as you would normally expect to do if you were on your own turf instead of in a television studio. In fact, such an exercise, carried out to its fullest potential, can do so much for your confidence that you might positively relish the prospect of an imminent video confrontation.

So effective is issues modelling that it seems a pity to confine its practice to emergencies or to those individuals who are most likely to be the company's television representatives. Increasingly, organizations are updating their issues models on a regular basis and conveying the statements that result throughout the management network. This is sound practice on several counts. First, the media will learn that no matter whom they ask for information and where they ask it—on the telephone, in the lounge bar, or outside the office—they will get the same answer. For the press, this is a distinct turn off. Much more interesting for the roving reporter is getting a variety of different or conflicting answers about the same topic within a corporation. That suggests confusion, or half-truths or—better still—outright lies. For a journalist, such a range of responses gives off the tell-tale scent of a juicy news story. A series of pre-determined, universally known and understood statements can be guaranteed to stop the news-hound's nose from twitching.

9
Looking beyond the notebook, the smile and the suntan

An assessment of the role of the television journalist/presenter. It is at once a job like any other and a job apart—with its own objectives, techniques, conventions, rewards and even a few hard and fast rules. Familiarity with what the television journalist wants and needs is half your battle won.

The preceding chapter ended with a particularly significant metaphor. Journalists were—quite conventionally—equated to dogs in their skills and behaviour. In other common English parlance reporters are frequently referred to as reptiles, leeches and vermin. None of these metaphors could be called terms of endearment. Rather, they are typical of the labels that one group of people assigns to another group whom they fear.

Recent polls indicate that as far as the general public is concerned, journalists are held in something less than lofty repute. Though they rank in popular esteem somewhat above double glazing salespeople and estate agents, they are nowhere near as trusted or respected as they once were.

There was a time, not all that long ago, when you believed what you read in the papers or watched on television. 'If they say it, it must be true', was the attitude of most of the reading and viewing public. Whether or not they were correct in their assumptions, or merely gullible, is immaterial. They thought they were getting the truth, and if not the whole story, then as much of it as they needed to make intelligent decisions. Those times are over.

Today, in the age of chequebook journalism, cheap sensationalism, page three smut, endemic invasion of privacy and downright journalistic bias, the pendulum has swung to the other extreme. The public believes little, if anything, it is told. This undoubtedly accounts for the size of the libel awards that juries now seem only too glad to grant against newspapers and television companies.

Yet there is a distinct danger in society's going too far in its condemnation of the press. If journalists are no longer the guardian angels of truth, neither are they some sort of sub-human life form. To think otherwise displays ignorance. The objective of the next few pages is to banish that ignorance, and replace it with an understanding of what the journalist wants, needs and expects.

What motivates a journalist? It is certainly not the money. Apart from a few nationally recognized figures who can command commensurate salaries, wages are, at best, merely adequate. More often, particularly on provincial papers and regional radio and television stations, they are modest to the point of parsimony. Expense accounts, once the stuff of legends, have gone the way of most overheads. Communications today is big business and no longer the hobby of rich and indulgent proprietors. Nor is the business of journalism intrinsically glamorous any more, as one pea-green television news reporter was quick to point out when doing a routine feature aboard a fishing vessel in the middle of a North Sea storm.

Prestige? Hardly. Those aforementioned libel suits—increasingly frequent, successful and costly—coupled with charges of invasion of privacy have done little lately for journalistic pride.

No. The answer must be that though journalists come in all shapes and sizes and degrees of literacy and honesty, they are different from the rest of us. They also differ from one another. Some, for instance, are of the school of the BBC's Jeremy Paxman, whose attitude to an interview subject appears to be 'Why is this lying swine lying to me?' Others are more receptive to their guests, particularly if they are celebrities. Jimmy Young, also of the BBC, has said that his reaction runs along the lines of 'Here am I, a baker's boy from Cinderford, talking to all these stars.'

Whether of the Paxman or Young schools of thought—or somewhere in between—television journalists have a mission, as they see it, to inform, disclose and, best of all wherever possible, to reveal. In a world of covert activities and black motives, they are the shedders of light. As such, they need a dark background against which to perform effectively. Good news, of the sort everyone else enjoys spreading, is hardly an effective way to set off their skills, except perhaps on Christmas Day or Good Friday, when nothing else seems to happen anyway.

For that reason, nothing makes a journalist happier than bad news. Does that make them ogres? Not at all. In private life, journalists not surprisingly display the usual range of human qualities including reticence and compassion. In their working lives, however, these qualities are necessarily subsumed. That is why a journalist's question, or a request for an interview, or an invitation to appear on television should immediately raise a red warning flag in your mind. Something, somewhere is wrong. The journalist thinks that you might have all or part of the story at your disposal or, at the very least, that you lead to someone who has. That is the journalist's job. Your job is to put the journalist's eagerness for a story to your own use.

But how does the journalist know so much already? Today, technology is firmly on the side of the information gatherers. Ten, or even five, years ago, just to learn the basics of your business would have taken hours of work in dusty archives. Now, a few strokes on the keyboard of the personal computer with which all reporters are equipped summons up screens of information that cover your organization, your industry and all the legislation that governs it.

That is not to say that the more traditional sources of information suffer from any neglect. Journalists also rely for story leads on reports from disgruntled employees and others who might have reason to be less than pleased with their compensation claims or redundancy settlements. You can be certain that they have lists of all your executives and managers, which were probably sold to them by someone in your mail room or copy centre. They undoubtedly have your in-house phone directory and a comprehensive and up-to-date organization chart.

Juicy information can also be obtained by stringers, those otherwise quite normal-looking people who hang about at pubs near the factory or perhaps mix the cocktails at the American Bar of the Savoy. When they are not shaking a sidecar or downing 'just the one' they are listening for and making note of all sorts of titbits. Most of what they acquire is a waste of their time. Some of it can prove to be very lucrative indeed. When they suspect they are on to something, they phone their agencies, who give them the green light and sometimes direct the way the story should go. Angles involving partners and children are always popular, since they make better pictures and human interest stories than do pin-striped business men.

In the wake of the Iraqi invasion of Kuwait, an oil company evacuated from neighbouring states the wives and children of expatriate employees. After a long and sometimes harrowing journey they arrived in Britain tired and under a great deal of emotional strain. The last thing they wanted was to run the gauntlet of the press. Therefore, in a discreet operation, they were taken to a quiet hotel in the country to recover from their ordeal. Within a day a reporter from the *Sun* was on the hotel doorstep. How did she find out about their presence? Perhaps a hotel maid or porter on the paper's payroll?

Company drivers are also frequently in the pay of the media. After all, they spend their days close to some of the most important people in the land. As drivers, they might not be paid terribly well. As stringers, they can earn a small fortune.

If all of these sources let down our intrepid reporters, they need not despair. They still have other information outlets to tap. A burglary, a violent crime, a fire or merely an accident involving an important member of the community is always worth a story. Fortunately for the spreaders of truth, the emergency services are not terribly well paid either. The police, firemen and ambulance drivers have been known to include moonlighters among their numbers. Even tradespeople—locksmiths, glaziers, cleaners, decorators—are not above suspicion. All are in a position to provide at least some aspect of a potentially interesting story to a grateful and perceptive journalist.

All of this information, collected during the course of what is for the journalist a normal working day, is saved up for a regular morning meeting at which the day's news output is planned. For television broadcasts, this meeting usually occurs at 10.00 am every day.

And guess what!

Today they have uncovered something interesting about your company. You discover this when you get a telephone call from a usually well-spoken, perhaps somewhat diffident, young woman. She will tell you her first name in a friendly sort of way, and you will assume that she must be a telephonist. This should be your first—and last—mistake in the conversation that follows. She is, in fact, either a researcher or one of the production team assigned to your story. She knows exactly what is going on and forms the advance guard of the media army now contemplating the prolonged siege of your privacy, your security and—if you let them—your sanity.

Inwardly, you should rush to your battle stations. Outwardly, you must be the voice of calm reason itself. Neither agree nor disagree to an interview, but politely turn the tables. (Just as you did in the earlier exercise with the newspaper reporter.) Ask her a few questions yourself. Why are they contemplating this story? (Do they know something you do not?) Who else will be interviewed? (You hardly want to confront the managing director who was sacked only last week.) Would the interview be live, or recorded, or the dreaded down-the-line in which you find yourself alone in a room with an automatic camera? Would they plan on showing any films, models or graphics? If so, could you see them in advance so that there are no surprises in the offing? What about visual aids you might want to provide?

Having had all your questions answered to your satisfaction, procrastinate. Tell the dulcet voice at the other end of the line that you will get back to her in 10 minutes. She will regard this as acquiescence, but that does not matter. Use the time to think. If you have access to public relations advice, ask about the track record of the journalists, producers, directors and presenters involved. Some are reputable and adhere to agreed criteria about areas of investigation. Others are shallow in their research and volatile in their on-camera presence.

After coolly assessing the invitation, you will naturally come to one of two decisions. If you decide that the risk of an appearance does not outweigh potential benefits, turn the invitation down, but do so carefully. Never give your real reasons. Instead, talk about pressure of work, bad timing, the unavailability at such short notice of the data you would require to perform effectively, conflicting engagements that you had hoped to get out of but could not, etc. She will have heard them all before, and you might detect just the hint of a chilly tone in the researcher's voice when you give these excuses, but that does not really matter.

On the other hand, if you decide that an appearance would be in your best interests as well as those of the organization and so accept the invitation, then there is no time to lose. Start on your homework and background preparation immediately to ensure that you come through the experience as you would wish to.

Meanwhile, back at the studio, time has not stood still either. After informing the meeting that you had already accepted the invitation (which you most certainly had not done at that premature stage, but never mind), the researcher or production assistant and her colleagues moved on to other topics. Your promised return telephone call jogs their memory, though they can't quite recall why they invited you in the first place. But that doesn't matter. They certainly have you now and they will make use of you. First, they will decide what storyline to follow at the interview. The angle they choose will be the one they think is the most interesting. This is inevitably the one that you would regard as most provocative. Such a tendency towards the sensational is known as editorializing, and journalists have every right to engage in the practice. After all, they are in the business of disclosure and revelation.

They are also in show business—or at least a branch of it. That means they must produce an element of drama before the camera to capture and keep their audience. And what does that audience like to see?

Use your empathetical skills yet once again. The primary television audience, you will recall, is the driver of the Clapham omnibus, complete with assorted relations, friends, neighbours and colleagues. A vapid and benign interview with the likes of you is hardly likely to interest or entertain them. A bit of confrontation, however, is something else entirely. After all, you are rather like the Clapham driver's boss, the person in control of the driver's life, free time, holidays, pay, security, self-esteem and all the rest. He or she would quite enjoy a couple of minutes of seeing the boss squirming uncomfortably in a television interview. Unfortunately, that is not likely to happen. However, if the bus depot supervisor is not available for an on-camera grilling, you provide an adequate substitute.

As for whoever might be doing the interviewing, he or she is busy in the run-up to your on-screen confrontation. How does a professional inquisitor go about such preparation? There is still a degree of mystery to this process. Brian Walden, for instance, is widely acknowledged as a master of his craft. David Cox of London Weekend Television, in his introduction to a volume of Walden interviews, describes how the star would take away a list of possible questions compiled by the researchers and

> ... in the hours that remained, pore over this, pacing about his room, until he had consigned its contents to some deep level of his consciousness. There they would fuse with his own instinctive attitudes and equip him to engage his interviewee without benefit of notes, in apparently spontaneous discourse.

On the other hand, according to Matthew Parris writing in *The Spectator*, when preparing for an interview on Weekend World, Walden

> ... would nip off to the bar, consign a packet of crisps and a drink to some deep level of his consciousness, chat about the state of the world with a cleaner and two lift-attendants, fuse a couple of cigarettes with his own instinctive attitudes, get a bit of a kip, wander in the next morning, blithely ignore the notes and still come up with a smashing interview.

Whichever is the more accurate description of the televisual journalistic process, the result is equally intimidating for the subject of the interview. As Walden himself puts it:

> Some of my best interviews have been with people who, in my heart of hearts, I don't like very much, and some of my worst have been with people of whom I am very fond.

When you think about it, that makes perfect sense. As far as entertainment and news value go, a spirited confrontation is virtually essential to a good interview.

And what about the rules of engagement? For the interviewers, for the most part, there are none. They can do what they like, though the BBC has paid lip service to certain behavioural restrictions in a series of guidelines, including recommendations about on-the-air behaviour. For example, BBC interviewers should '... avoid impressions of bias through tone and inflection or through careless wording which seems to disorientate an interviewee—"Are you in this mess because you are stupid or just foolish?"—and which are out of place on the BBC. They are likely to be as counterproductive as they are discourteous.'

Discourtesy might be banned at the BBC, but the rest of the arsenal of interview weapons remains at the disposal of the smooth talker with the clipboard as a shield.

This, then, is what you have let yourself in for: the late twentieth century equivalent of a gladiatorial circus. Yet you do not go into combat unarmed:

- You have done your homework.
- You have prepared your model and practised reductive communication to distil the essential statements you want to get across.
- You are firmly inculcated with the vital importance of the second personal pronoun.
- You have purged your mind of jargon.
- You are a fountainhead of lively, pertinent and original imagery to illustrate your ideas.

You are ready.

10
Bright lights, potted plants, make-up and you

In which you make your acquaintance with the alien, indifferent and perhaps even hostile environment of a television studio. You learn about the mechanics of the operation and its ancillaries. Who will you see? What do they do? Why? There are points to score and pitfalls to avoid. The most sophisticated, high-powered international executive who ventures into a studio without the necessary foreknowledge has no better chance of coming out intact than a lamb entering an abattoir.

Try to remember the way you used to feel at school or university when you were on your way to sit an important examination. A great deal was riding on your performance, so you were prepared. Though your mind might have been crammed full of every question you could conceivably face, together with the answers you would give, you were not exactly over-confident. After all, anything could happen.

Nevertheless, you were pretty certain you had done your necessary homework. As you arrived at the examination hall, it was with that slight high that comes just before your adrenalin begins to pump. Having done all you could beforehand, you were almost looking forward to getting the ordeal over with. On the other hand, what if you suddenly went blank? Such things do happen. Perhaps that fear accounted for the sudden hyperactivity of your bladder or bowels.

If you can conjure up something akin to what you felt back then (remember the Actors' Studio technique?), you can come close to anticipating your reaction to your first television interview. There are, however, a few differences to note. For one, a failure at examinations would have been a fairly private matter, of importance only to you, your tutor and perhaps your parents. Failure on television is, by definition, a public humiliation. In other words, you are playing for much higher stakes indeed.

Timing is another important difference. When sitting an examination, the test begins when the invigilator says it does, and not a moment before. Until then, you can relax—as far as is possible—and trade jokes, last-minute question predictions and plausible answers with anyone around you. There is a degree of comfort in any mass ordeal.

When undergoing a television interview, the trial begins the moment you set foot in the studio car park—or even before if the studio has been kind enough to send a car for you. From that moment on, you are on alien territory, and should be careful to behave accordingly for one simple reason: there are news gatherers all around you. Your friendly studio driver, for instance. How do you know that he is not a reporter? The same holds true for the uniformed guard at the door. And what about a harmless banter with that devastatingly attractive receptionist? Flirt at your peril.

At a television studio, the wisdom behind a venerable psychiatric joke most definitely applies: 'Just because you happen to be a paranoid schizophrenic, it does not necessarily hold true that you are *not* being followed.'

Having run the gauntlet of studio driver, security guard and receptionist, your interview experience really begins to take off. You will now be met be a bright and chipper young thing who will express the television company's gratitude for your time and your willingness to speak to them. She—and it usually will be a young woman—will do great things for your ego. She will find you and your job absolutely fascinating and will probably inundate you with flattering questions. Beware. She might give every indication of being someone's rather charming secretary. She is not. Instead, she is part of the production team, and her brief is to find out even more about you and your interview topic than the researchers know already. She is very skilful at this.

And what is your normal reaction when you are being flattered? You preen, of course, but you also feel the need to go in for self-deprecation just to show that the flattery is not really going to your head. After all, you are not that sort of person. So, to prove that you really are nothing special, you belittle yourself a bit and just for good measure, perhaps, you also denigrate your job and the organization you represent. You do your best to show that there are flaws behind the perfect façade you are apparently presenting to this enraptured creature.

Without this forewarning, you would probably never realize what is going on. The technique involved is very subtle. But at this stage, with a careless comment or what might seem an innocuous joke to break the ice, you could succeed in sabotaging your own television debut.

If, when you arrive at the studio, there is some time to spare—and there usually seems to be—your first stop through the looking glass in video land could be what is grandly known as 'the hospitality suite' or, in continuation of a theatrical convention dating back to the eighteenth century, 'The Green Room'. (It is invariably any shade but green.) Here, amidst the half-empty styrofoam cups and the overflowing ashtrays, you might well find a series of plaques affixed to the walls above the chairs that ring the room. 'In this chair sat HRH The Duke of Edinburgh', one might read. Another chair might celebrate a temporary acquaintance with the posterior of The Right Honourable Margaret Thatcher. In any case, such notices and a range of signed and framed celebrity photos on the wall are not exactly designed to put a novice like you at your ease. 'What on earth am *I* doing here?' you quite rightly ask yourself. You are now feeling highly intimidated, as no doubt you were meant to do.

How do you recover your self-respect? If possible, have a sympathetic (but discreet) friend or colleague accompany you to the studio. This will ensure that you do not suffer from that feeling of isolation that can wear you down and make you talkative. If you must be on your own, be prepared for the initimidating solitude. Take some notes with you to study or, if last minute cribbing makes you even more nervous, go prepared with a book or magazine. Whatever you do, do not let any temporary loneliness loosen your tongue to the detriment of your interview.

Nor should you give in to another obvious temptation: drink. Perhaps never in your life will you feel a greater need for a comforting swig. The studio knows this and, their profits permitting, you are likely to find a tempting drinks tray laid out for your delectation. Resist the urge for anything stronger than a tonic water. Too many unwary guests (including professional celebrities who should have known better) have succumbed to nerves in the hospitality suite, only to find all their preparation—not to mention their useful inhibitions—dangerously diluted by alcohol by the time they reached the camera.

Once the studio powers that be feel that you have been sufficiently softened up by a stint in their equivalent of the hot box, someone will be along to suggest that you do a run-through with the interview presenter. This you cannot reasonably refuse. You can, however, politely decline to give the game away, which is what the presenter is after.

As the interviewer rabbits on, listen attentively. By all means nod if you like, but do not say much beyond the odd affirmative or two that yes, you can answer that question. *Never* give any indication as to what that answer might be. There are a number of reasons for this reticence at this stage in the proceedings. For one, if you actually answer a question at this point, you will inevitably have a feeling of *déjà vu* later on during the actual on-camera interview. To avoid this uncomfortable sensation, the mind usually forces the tongue to reword the answer and mess it up in the process. Your first answer to a question is invariably your best. Do not waste your best response in a mere practice session.

If you do answer a question at this stage, and it is asked again, you also run the risk of harking back to your off-camera conversation. You might well respond 'As I said earlier . . .' or 'I can only repeat . . .'. These are natural prefaces to a question asked the second time around. However, such responses are, at best, confusing to the viewer, who has not had the privilege of seeing your earlier, practice interview. It can also suggest a degree of collusion between you and the presenter which undercuts the whole point of the confrontation.

Worst of all though, is the risk you run of giving so complete, so thorough, so irrefutable a response to the question, that your presenter is warned off the topic entirely. A foolproof answer on your part makes your presenter look foolish. If he or she knows that risk in advance, in the privacy of the Green Room, you are hardly likely to be asked the same question a second time, in full view of millions of witnesses.

The other thing to guard against is forming a rapport—or what you might regard as a rapport—with your inquisitor. He or she might well prove to be highly agreeable, not a stuck-up media celebrity at all. The presenter does his or her best to put you at ease and you might find yourself grateful for this solicitous attention. Do not give in to that sensation of gratitude. The more relaxed you find yourself with your interviewer, the more you are likely to let down your defences. Be pleasant and polite, by all means, but be on your guard, as well. What you are reading as convivial friendliness is merely another part of the television presenter's job. As far as he or she is concerned, you are nothing more or less than interview fodder. Remember that, and you will not go far wrong in any preliminary sessions.

Once you have been dumped by the production assistant, and the presenter has finished with you, your interaction with the studio staff suddenly seems to come to an end. At this point, loneliness might prevail once more. At a loss for anything to do, you might be tempted to wander out into the studio itself. By all means do so. There, you will see dozens of people in varying stages of activity or inertia. You might even feel the urge to engage in a bit of harmless small talk with one or two of them. Once again, resist what in any other environment would be a harmless human predilection.

There is a reason for this prescribed reticence. Pity the poor camera operator, for instance, who is minding his own business and working through the shot lists he receives from the director. Though video cameras might be your undying private passion, the studio camera operator does not want to hear about it. He has heard about it all before. Hundreds of times. Nor does he want to answer your questions about what camera he is using and why. Your empathetical skills should tell you that he has been exposed to that same tired conversational ploy by every lonely visitor who has ever wandered through the studio. Least of all does he want to give you advice on how your favourite nephew might break into the business. At that nadir of your monologue, he will simply walk away. To avoid that humiliating experience, confine your conversational exchange with the camera operator to a polite 'Good day', followed by a request for help in finding the floor manager. The camera operator will be impressed. It tells him you know what you are about.

Of all the people you see milling about a television studio, the floor manager is the one and only person who is actually paid to look after you. As far as he or she is concerned, you are as important as—but no more important than—any other prop the production might require. That is not to say that the floor manager is callous. It is also the floor manager's responsibility to make sure that the lights do not burn your eyes and that you are comfortable. He or she will go on to sort out the audio levels for the recording. The jargon for this (and they are allowed to use their jargon, since they are on home base) will be 'Can we have a level?', followed by the seemingly irrelevant question of what you had for breakfast. Your answer should be confined to few simple sentences delivered in a normal conversational tone. Do not attempt to be helpful by counting aloud, 'Testing: one, two, three . . .', etc. This would only cause the sound meter to swing uselessly to overload and back again.

The floor manager is also the person you will see giving the 'cue' sign and hand signals for 'half way', 'wind up' and the rather threatening gesture to the throat that indicates 'cut'. When giving these signals, the floor manager is not acting on his or her own initiative, but merely following the directions of the producer and the director, both of whom are ensconced in the gallery or control room. The headset worn by the floor manager is linked to their control panel.

LOOKING THE PART

Sooner or later you will have an important decision to make: to be or not to be made up. There should be no question in your mind at all. You *will* be made up for your television debut, no matter what your scruples about powder and paint. Modern television make-up serves a variety of functions. Most important, it stops you from sweating under the hot television lights.

To watch someone sweating is not a pleasant sight. It looks almost as uncomfortable as it feels. What is worse, however, is what we associate with a dripping forehead, a shining nose and a glistening chin. An individual who is sweating on camera looks as though he or she is lying—particularly if those who share the eye of the camera simultaneously appear cool, calm and collected. If any further evidence is required, simply remember what Richard Nixon looked like on his television appearances. The Nixon–Kennedy debates marked a turning point in television history.

For the first time, the power of the medium became apparent. Those who followed the debates on radio were convinced that Nixon swept the floor with Kennedy. The majority of American voters, however, followed the action on television. Nixon eschewed make-up and, ultimately, the nation eschewed him.

Television make-up also helps to give a degree of consistency to skin tone. Since neither lighting nor cameras are adjusted for different television subjects (unless you are a star), a refusal to wear make-up can make you look either pallid or florid. What is worse, any minor broken blood vessels or spots which, in normal life, would attract little if any notice, on television take on monumentally revolting proportions. If your complexion is naturally fresh, you could even end up looking dangerously drunk, which is particularly ironic if you exercised discipline over the Green Room drinks tray.

Women particularly should consent to a professional studio make-up job. The perfection of their everyday *maquillage* notwithstanding, street make-up simply cannot stand up to the rigours of studio lighting. At best, it looks grotesque. At worst, it can begin to run, thereby providing an element of fascinating, if distracting, drama for the home television audience.

To restate the obvious, television is primarily a visual medium. Therefore, what you look like is as important—and perhaps even more important—than anything you might have to say. Women tend to understand this better than men, since—at least until very recently—women have been taught that appearance is their most important attribute. Men, on the other hand, have been taught the opposite. 'You can't tell a book by its cover' was a cliché seldom applied to women, often to men. Perhaps these differing cultural attitudes have brought about the standard reaction when people are first exposed to video tapes of their television appearances. Men most often express disbelief at the way they sound. Women have an initial shock about the way they look. In a way, this surprise is understandable. Having spent years looking at yourself in a mirror and so becoming used to seeing yourself merely in reflection, it can come as a shock to see yourself exactly as you appear to other people, thanks to the magic of television optics.

Television tends to play other tricks on women as well. For one, it highlights their culturally imposed tendency to placate. In Western society, women are generally seen as peacemakers. It is their perceived role to defuse conflict, to smooth ruffled feathers. Oddly, this is true even for those women who in other sectors of their lives are seen as otherwise active, aggressive or even intimidating. The BBC's senior reporter Kate Adie provides a perfect example. As part of her job and at great personal risk, she has fearlessly covered wars, insurrections, retaliatory attacks and just about every nasty situation that has occurred anywhere in the world in the past 10 years. Nevertheless, out of her usual reporter's role, and in the informal context of a network chat show interview, she has been known to come across as reserved to the point of diffidence, reverting to the feminine television stereotype when faced with an unfamiliar studio situation.

Yet again, Mrs Thatcher provides another prime—even former Prime Ministerial—example. Hers is hardly the typical feminine public image. As a politician and party leader, she was perceived as strong, unswerving and perhaps even ruthless in her single-mindedness. Nevertheless, despite these attributes, and even after she assumed the mantle of a latter-day Boadicea following the Falklands victory, Mrs Thatcher as Prime Minister still had a marked tendency to succumb to a number of conventionally feminine failings in her television appearances.

Her frequent smile was often terrible to behold, since it seldom matched the mood or tone of the message she was trying to put across. For the viewer, this was disconcerting and occasionally even sinister. Her voice, too, presented a problem, as do the voices of most women on television. Because of differences in modulation, a woman engaged in active conversation on camera tends to sound over-excited and undisciplined on what is generally regarded as a 'cool' medium. This is, of course, horribly unfair, but it remains a fact and one that Mrs Thatcher obviously came to acknowledge. Over the years, she put a great deal of effort into lowering her voice to obliterate effectively the contrast in tone between her and her inquisitors. In this she was successful, albeit at the expense of spontaneity. By lowering her modulation, she invariably sounded studied in her pronouncements.

Given the significance of the visual on television, there are a few simple guidelines to be followed on overall appearance, but these are refreshingly non-sexist and universally applicable. For instance, before a television appearance anyone—man or woman—should give some serious consideration to wardrobe.

This is not as frivolous as it might first seem. Though the modern camera can cope with any colour or lighting situation, some colours are better than others. Red, for instance, has the unfortunate tendency to bleed and blotch. Basic black and white, which *sounds* as though it should work, does not. The stark contrast can cause the camera to close down electronically in compensation for the reflection from white fabric. For that reason, pastel colours tend to appear best—with the probable exception of pale blue. In the early 1970s Ted Heath learnt colour recommendation to his cost. He appeared in a television interview resplendent in a party politically correct light blue ensemble that unfortunately merged precisely into the chroma-key background used for showing television graphics. As a result, the Prime Minister of the United Kingdom literally disappeared before the nation's eyes in a suit that suddenly seemed to sprout intriguing patterns never before associated with Savile Row tailoring. Given the famous Heath grin, the experience was akin to watching a Tory Cheshire Cat slowly disappear—except of course for that memorable and enduring smile.

Ted Heath learnt that particular lesson well. The ex-Prime Minister now mostly wears pale grey for his less frequent television appearances.

Other fabrics can cause other problems. Unless you were appearing on camera with Dame Edna Everage (a situation to be avoided at all costs) you would hardly sport gold or silver lamé for a typical television interview. This is just as well since those fabrics, together with satin, some polyester blends and sequin embroidery all tend to strobe blindingly, particularly on older video equipment. More insidiously, however, so does corduroy. Even a discreet Prince of Wales check can start throbbing under the cameras, thereby distracting the driver of the Clapham omnibus from what you are saying to what you are wearing—which is not the point of your appearance at all.

Similarly distracting can be things that clink and shine such as large earrings or brooches or necklaces. Occasionally, with rings or bracelets on a dramatically gesticulating arm, a phenomenon called 'cometing' occurs and the startled viewer suddenly sees a shooting star flash across the screen.

Another glare to be avoided if at all possible concerns men exclusively. Few things are more unappealing than the expanse of shiny white shin between the cuffs of too-short trousers and the tops of too-short socks. It is a sight that stupidly succeeds in distracting from the significance of any topic being discussed.

And speaking of sights, spectacles can be another cause for concern. If you need them, so be it. However, you should be aware that they create yet another barrier between you and your audience. Just think of the layers of glass that separate you from them: the television screen, the camera lens, and your spectacles. Each of those serves to minimize to a small degree the projection of your personality. 'The eyes are the windows of the soul', the Victorians liked to believe. Perhaps they were right. And perhaps one of the reasons that John Major must labour under the 'grey man' label is the dominance of the large, rectangular spectacles that he wears in every television appearance.

If glasses are essential, be sure they hide your eyes as little as possible, which means foreswear any spectacles that darken with exposure to light. These photosensitive lenses not only cause great problems to the technicians who are trying to keep you in the most favourable light, they also succeed in completely hiding your eyes. As a result, you assume a guilty countenance resembling nothing less than a mobster about to be indicted on a morals charge.

Spectacles can provide another problem, as well. Often, they become a personal prop, to be played with in moments of stress or anxiety. Prime Minister Alec Douglas Home learnt this to his great cost in 1964 when he narrowly lost the general election to Harold Wilson. A quarter-century later, recalling her husband's famous half-moon spectacles, Lady Home of the Hirsel would recount: 'Oh, you want to hear about the glasses . . . the reason Alec lost the general election. It wasn't just that he wore them, but that he kept taking them off and putting them on. It didn't go down well on television. And 1964, you must remember, was the first real television election in this country. Am I not right, Alec?'. 'You usually are', replied her husband.

Hats can provide another danger area, though there is no television lore about the loss of an election due to one—with the possible exception of a New York mayoral campaign in the early 1970s, when candidate Bella Abzug insisted on wearing a huge picture hat for every appearance. The fact is that on television, the wearing of a hat should always be avoided, for men and women alike. A woman wearing a hat on television conjures up images of Ascot or a garden party—perfectly acceptable occasions in themselves perhaps but oddly jarring in an interview to those at home sitting slumped before the television. For this reason, feathers are absolutely out.

A man wearing a hat is equally distracting and, depending on his choice of headgear, can instantly antagonize a huge segment of his audience. One of the most enduringly destructive images after the Zeebrugge disaster was a director of P&O European Ferries being interviewed beneath the insouciant brim of a tweed fishing hat. It did not enhance either his image or, more importantly, that of his company.

Despite all these caveats, your objective before the cameras is to look as natural as possible. Ironically, the only way you can achieve this natural look is through an almost unhealthy preoccupation with your appearance. Before the cameras begin to roll, check for any of the minute flaws that the eye normally filters out as irrelevant, but which the camera will magnify to the point of absurdity. Your hair should be neat and free of any dandruff or fluff. Your collar and shoulders (the only bits that show in the usual No. 1 shot) should be similarly pristine. Smooth any wrinkles in your shirt and jacket and ensure that your jacket is resting properly on your shoulders. If you are sitting down, it is a good idea to unbutton your jacket, since if left fastened, it will stand away from your neck. Any tie or scarf should be neatly in place, even if it is merely what Mrs Thatcher, in an interview on Prime Ministerial style, fondly referred to as 'something soft at the neck'.

And speaking of Mrs Thatcher yet again, it is worth analysing any subliminal messages that your choice of wardrobe might be transmitting. For some observers, the apotheosis of Mrs Thatcher's power came at her last Prime Ministerial appearance at the Lord Mayor's Banquet. Her arrival at the Guildhall was naturally covered by television. As she emerged from her car she appeared as a modern approximation of Gloriana, wearing a long dress complete with train (which had to be arranged by a woman looking suspiciously like a lady in waiting) and a large white ruff framing her face. The Greeks have a word for choosing to appear in such a costume—at least as it looked on television. And that word is hubris. By appearing to assume the mantle of Tudor royalty, Mrs Thatcher overreached herself. Moreover, she did so in full sight of millions of her countrymen and women. From that moment on, her fall from power was not in question. Only its timing was still to be determined and that came a mere three weeks later.

On television what finishing schools refer to as deportment is also important. Your body language, the way in which you occupy that less than capacious hot seat in the studio, speaks volumes to the viewer. Above all, try to avoid what media consultant Sandra Dickinson aptly refers to as the 'Widow Twankey position', with belly distended and ankles crossed. This, she cautions, 'fixes the eyes most unfortunately on the genitals', which, depending of course on the subject under discussion, is hardly likely to put forward your argument.

Your gestures are also something of which you should be aware. Some people use body language more than others and, certainly, there is nothing intrinsically wrong with arm and hand movements to emphasize and punctuate your oral communication. However, on television these should be kept within control. Stage actors who also do television work quickly learn that what is effective in reaching the back row of the stalls becomes laughably artificial in front of a television camera. The small screen calls for discreet movement that occurs at a slower than usual pace, since the television camera has the tendency to accelerate ordinary movement.

Whatever subtle and measured gestures you feel compelled to make before the camera, keep your hands away from your face. If you forget this you risk casting bizarre shadows across your visage, which is distraction enough. But worse than that, the camera will magnify even the most delicate digits and make your hand look like a grotesquely animated bunch of bananas.

Whatever you do with your hands, and no matter how nervous you might be, resist the temptation to smoke. Rightly or wrongly, smoking in public is now seen as an unforgivable social sin. On television, it certainly is. Health grounds apart, it inevitably puts your hands between your face and the camera. Even worse, the smoke you exhale has a habit of lingering around you and your on-camera companions, creating a distinctly distracting ambience more reminiscent of a Soho jazz club than a television studio. Forget any vestiges of glamour that you might still associate with on-screen smoking from films of the 1940s. Though it might once have been acceptable, today it simply does not work on television.

Those vital trivialities out of the way, it is worth examining the forms your television interview might take.

KNOWING THE SCORE

The most typical interview set-up is the one-to-one situation with a presenter in a television studio. This has come to be the UK convention for both the BBC and ITV, as well as the newly proliferating satellite and cable stations. In this interview format you do what comes naturally by looking at your interlocutor throughout.

Almost as popular is the panel interview—either with or without a studio audience. In this case, your attention should follow whoever is talking—either the interviewer, a fellow panel member, or a member of the audience posing a question.

By far the trickiest and—unfortunately an increasingly common—interview format is what is known as 'down-the-line'. It is most often used at fairly short notice, usually to give background to an item on a regular news bulletin. Technology is all when it comes to down-the-line. You are told to report to either a very small studio with a single camera and its operator or, worse still, you experience something more akin to a railway station passport photo booth featuring a television camera remotely controlled from another location by a joystick. In either case, your interviewer is miles away at the television centre. You are linked there either by a tied GPO line or a microdish.

Though the interviewer can see you well enough on studio monitors, you cannot see the interviewer. But you can hear a disembodied voice through a plug jammed in your ear and resembling a primitive device for the deaf. As your interview begins, you will hear yourself being introduced. At this point, make sure you nod in acknowledgement. If not, there will be a horrible few moments for all concerned when the interviewer—and the audience—wonder whether or not you are actually connected to the system. It has been known to happen that an unfortunate guest spends an interminable 30 seconds or so staring straight ahead, waiting for that eternity before hearing the first question—which, due to technical faults, never comes.

However, even when all goes well from a technical point of view, down-the-line is an unusual and unnerving position in which to find yourself. Nevertheless, it is one that must be mastered. An effective way to do this is by training yourself at home to talk to an alarm clock on the kitchen table. This otherwise certifiable habit should get you accustomed to speaking in an animated fashion without the benefit or encouragement of any human feedback at all. The trick is to look either directly at the lens (or alarm clock, if you are practising) or down at the notes you have placed on your lap, preferably on the back of one of your business cards which you can hold in the palm of your hand. Look neither up in the air nor down to the ground and *never* look to the left or to the right. This panning movement with the eyes creates a decidedly reptilian appearance and inevitably makes you look devious. Once again, think back to the television performances of Richard Nixon and you will be suitably chastened.

Because it is difficult to look directly into the lens for any great length of time, have no hesitation in breaking your otherwise basilisk gaze and look down momentarily to your notes. Then look up and say something. Then repeat the process. This gives your viewers as much of a welcome break as it does you.

Throughout the process, remember to sit upright, lean forward into the lens and sit square—however unnatural all of this might feel. The reason behind this is simple: the television set itself is level and angular. By leaning sideways to any degree your movement appears exaggerated because it breaks the perpendicularity of the frame. As a result, you will look as though you are falling over. While this might well amuse the driver of the Clapham omnibus and family, it will do nothing for your credibility in their less-than-sympathetic eyes.

The one interview situation in which you might expect a bit of sympathy—at least initially—is the dreaded 'doorstep'. This is the format for which you cannot plan, except in the general sense. It usually occurs following an emergency of one sort or another and can take place anywhere you might find yourself: at the airport, outside a courtroom, leaving a train or station, outside your office or even (perish the thought) just beyond the sanctity and security of your own front door.

The first and foremost rule for such encounters—for that is exactly what they are—is to stand stock still. You can be certain that from the moment you first spotted the small news team with their news-gathering camera, that camera was rolling away. Any attempt at evasion on your part will be shown whether or not they succeed in getting any more out of you. And the sight of anyone running away from the camera—or worse still slamming the door on it—leaves an indelible stain of video guilt on that unfortunate person's reputation. And how could it be any other way? Given the protocols of television, a rejection of the camera (or worse still, Esther Rantzen or one of her acolytes) is an automatic rejection of the viewer himself. No one forgives or forgets such rejection.

So, having resolved to make the best of a sorry situation, give your impromptu interview as best and as graciously as you can. When you and the crew have finished, stand your ground. Do not even begin to move until the crew begins to pack the camera away. If you do, and the editor is unscrupulous, you could find yourself apparently running away on the nine o'clock news despite all your valiant efforts to the contrary.

Preparing yourself for the ordeal of doorstepping is difficult. Fortunately, familiarizing yourself with the other interview formats and their environments is considerably easier. Most local television stations are fairly hospitable places—unless you are being interviewed. A civilized letter to the news editor (addressed by name) followed up by an equally civilized telephone call should do the trick. After all, the time could arise when they need you as much as you need them.

Having once visited a station on a reconnaissance mission, much of what you have read in this chapter will quickly fall into place. The courtesies, the protocols, the disciplines and the technology will lose some, if not all, of their mystique. Before long, you will feel considerably more confident in using television to your own advantage, like any other piece of office machinery or electronic gadgetry. That is as it should be; particularly as you gird your discreetly pale-grey clad loins to put all you have learnt about television techniques to the test of your first interview.

11
In the den of the video lion

At long last you are on camera, under fire. The rules of the television interview technique, if followed implicitly, convert you from harried potential victim into cool, calm and confident master of the medium. All you need to do at this stage is learn a few basic points and then make them your own. Once these become second nature to you, nothing can go wrong.

There was a time—not so very long ago by normal standards, but back in the Palaeolithic Age as far as television is concerned, during the BBC 1 broadcast monopoly—when interviews were of the fireside chat variety. They were warm and cosy: polite exchanges between gentlemen of fairly equal social standing, educational background and professional distinction. They dressed alike, they spoke alike, and by and large they even thought alike.

On the morning following one of these less than intense encounters, there would be great interest in the studio about the content of the programme and a discussion on exactly what had been said and what the implications of that exchange of ideas might be. The whole concept was intentionally low key and seriously informative.

Then things changed. The debut of alternative television channels spurred the competition for audiences that dominates the industry today. This is highly understandable. For the independent television companies, viewing figures translated directly into advertising revenues. If they attracted more of an audience they could charge more for their commercial space. The BBC, no longer a monopoly, had to justify its existence—and its quickly escalating licence fees—by expanding its viewer franchise. The brief was no longer the nobly Reithian dictum to educate, inform and edify, but to entertain as well. The old interview techniques, sound as they were in a gentler era, no longer applied. To get popular audiences, the television companies had to use popular methods: television journalism and television entertainment were to become interchangeable concepts.

Craig Brown, writing on television for *The Times*, described the evolution in a particularly colourful way:

> As late as the seventies, it [television] had counterfeited the air of a servant, still listening through the door rather than barging in bold as brass, still accepting its position with a deferential nod. But now it snaps its fingers and we all come running.
>
> In the eighties, the two world powers both chose television personalities for President. The Labour Party elected a leader largely because he had made a good impression on television, so did the Social and Liberal Democrats. Even the most standoffish learnt to bend their knees in service of the box: first The Lords, and then The Commons, and, each year, a new member of the Royal Family.
>
> In the seventies, the Royal Family had let a partial light in on their magic by allowing themselves to be filmed barbecuing, sharing a joke with Heads of State, and acting normal in a slightly exaggerated way. But in the eighties, there was no stopping them: one minute, Prince Andrew was flirting with Selina Scott; the next, Princess Anne was changing her image on Wogan. Prince Charles became a more democratic version of Alan Whicker; the Duchess of York plugged her children's books with Sue Lawley; and Princess Michael of Kent chose breakfast television as a forum to answer allegations about her father's Nazi past. Prince Edward organised 'It's a Royal Knockout', in which junior members of the Royal Family dressed up as oldeworlde Kings and Queens and leapt about in tubs of vanilla blanc mange; and, in the final year of the decade, a previously discreet and minor member of the Royal Family could be seen choking back her tears as she moaned about her parents on a daily worries programme run by a softly spoken former Labour MP: 'Take a deep breath, Marina'.

Of course, not everyone joined in the fun willingly. At least one member of the Royal Family, Princess Margaret, remained nostalgic for a degree of diffidence from the media. She was among the guests at a gala National Film Theatre showing of a newly-restored tape of the earliest television coverage of a coronation—that of her parents. The evening's commentator remarked on the long-shot coverage of the coronation carriage, its occupants barely discernible, and pointed out that this distance was not so much a technical limitation as a conscious sign of respect on the part of the BBC. 'Quite right, too', intoned the royal mezzo-soprano from her seat in the back row.

Princess Margaret's opinions notwithstanding, the very highest level of society clearly not only acquiesced to the change in television, but actually conspired in it. It is hardly surprising that since then television has consistently lowered both its sights and its standards. Not that it was difficult to do so, particularly in what had been considered the most sacrosanct of all television activities: coverage of the news.

Using an increasingly raunchy popular press as their model, the television moguls focused on an idea of video news very different from that of their mentors in the BBC and the earlier days of ITN. Morbid sensationalism is the essence of this commercially evolved television news philosophy.

Admittedly, it does have a sound foundation. After all, in their private lives, people do not sing the praises of their happily married neighbours. Instead, they talk among their friends of those marriages on the verge of break-up. Even Tolstoy recognized the human fascination for domestic troubles. His *Anna Karenina* begins with the astute observation that 'All happy families are alike. Every unhappy family is unhappy in its own way.'

Similarly, it is the unique quality of non-domestic strife and misfortune that people find appealing. They do not talk about good drivers; they talk about fatal accidents. They do not focus on industrial successes. They want to hear about industrial mistakes—the bigger and more embarrassing, like Union Carbide's at Bhophal, the better.

Nor should journalists be strictly censured for this. They merely earn their livings by catering to what is, after all, a universal human trait. The Germans have a good word for it: *Schadenfreude*. It means joy in other people's misery, or—to revert to a previous image—the exquisite feeling experienced by the driver of the Clapham omnibus when he or she can watch the boss, or at least a boss substitute, squirm. That is why, when you agree to give an interview, you can expect trouble. It is what modern television broadcasting is all about.

Fortunately, trouble expected should mean trouble averted.

You are already equipped with the three essential skills in effective televisual communication:

- Attracting attention
- Retaining attention
- Leaving a message

What is more, you are familiar with journalistic motivations and with the physical set-up you can expect in a studio or down-the-line interview.

Having anticipated the tone any television interview is likely to take, there are three simple rules for coping with the professional (not personal) hostility you are likely to encounter in an interview.

RULE ONE: *Get across your predetermined message.*

Any interview is as much your opportunity to be heard as the interviewer's—perhaps more so. Therefore, you should not have agreed to submit yourself to on-camera quizzing unless you yourself have something you want to say. That being the case, use the time before you leave the office to isolate your points in your own mind.

Remember that, in all, you might have only about 15 seconds in which to get your message across. What can you possibly say in that ridiculous span of time? Not a great deal, admittedly. But if you distil your ideas into two or three statements, a quarter-minute is ample time, provided you enter the fray with the determination to make those points, come what may.

As an extra bit of discipline, write those two or three sentences on the back of your business card and keep the card in the palm of your hand. Look at it repeatedly in the lead-up to the interview and, if necessary, force yourself to glance down at the card during the interview itself.

Whatever happens, know those points and give voice to them.

RULE TWO: *Let nothing go by default.*

Civilized people are taught from their earliest years to turn the other cheek in response to offensive remarks. The rules of civilized behaviour are, by and large, suspended for the duration of any television interview.

There is a good reason for this. A professional television presenter rightly regards every interview as a possible challenge to hard-earned authority and popularity and, ultimately, career success. A boring interview, one with no sparkle, one in which the guest (you) seems to be getting an easy ride is regarded by the interviewer and his or her colleagues as an ignoble failure. Too many of those and the poor presenter could end up doing nothing more glamorous than covering warehouse fires and the less interesting picket lines.

Therefore, to keep things nice and bouncy and, above all, entertaining the skilled interviewer will challenge you in as rude and outrageous a way as necessary. If someone tried that on you in an ordinary social situation, you would have three choices. You could get up and leave, maintain a dignified and dismissive silence or—if really provoked—give vent to either verbal or physical violence. However, as you will have gathered by now, television is anything but a normal social situation. Silence on your part in the face of aggressive provocation comes across to the viewer as only one thing: tacit agreement.

Instead of just sitting there if something is said with which you cannot agree, say so. Loudly and insistently. Depending on the mood and tone of the interview, your aural disassociation from the presenter's comment can range from a firm 'no' to a somewhat more assertive 'That's just not so' to the more dismissive cry of 'nonsense' or 'rubbish!' And whatever you might say or do, discipline yourself away from the conventionally polite gesture of nodding in agreement with whatever your conversational partner might say. In real life this is an endearing habit, since it encourages your partner in discourse. On television, it can put you in the moronic position of seeming to agree with a view diametrically opposed to your own.

RULE THREE: *Keep off other people's business.*

You have your own agenda in any television interview, and getting those points across is sufficiently challenging to absorb all your energy and attention. Why, then, waste time and effort in commenting on anyone else's affairs?

Of course, you should not, but television presenters like you to do so. For one, it makes their jobs easier. After all, you are an expert on your topic. They are not. If they can get you off the specific and into generalities, they recover some of the advantage. But, as you will have gathered by now, you are never on anything approaching even ground with a television presenter. He or she is playing on home territory. And so, once you are off your area of expertise, you are at the interviewer's mercy—a quality strained at the best of times.

It is all too easy to find yourself trapped in details about which you know little, if anything. Suddenly, you could find yourself embroiled in someone else's problem. Though it is laudable, in other circumstances, to come to the support of colleagues in your industry or discipline, on television such valour is akin to suicide. Nor is it your responsibility to answer for the actions of an adversary or competitor. When posed such a question, simply say, 'You had better ask so-and-so', and then come back to the point *you* are trying to make.

These three rules evolved in the early 1970s, alongside the three essential skills isolated by observation of army broadcasters. Since then, they have been put into application by thousands of business executives, politicians, members of the police and armed forces and more than a few royal personages.

When put into practice properly they are foolproof.

Nevertheless, it is worth while to examine more closely how these simple rules, combined with the basic skills, are best brought into play during an interview.

MAKING THE MOST OF YOUR BRIEF ENCOUNTER

A television interview is hardly a school for conventionally good behaviour. As already pointed out, the rules of civilized society are left behind in the Green Room with the cigarette ends and the coffee dregs. What you are left with is a set of peculiar conventions that—at least on camera—take on the illusion of normal restraints and acceptable or at least unexceptional manners.

The constraints of television time provide a prime example. Most normal conversations operate in a leisurely, rambling, give-and-take sequence of exchanges. Even if you seriously disagree with someone, you give that person time to explain his or her position, and expect that no less than the same courtesy be shown to you. On television, however, there is no time to explain anything—which is why you have reduced your explanations to simple, straightforward statements. Instead, questions are fired at you with machine gun speed, and you have no time to deal with them properly—or even individually. But that does not matter. The interviewer is merely following an editorialized storyline anyway. Any real answers to questions would only slow that storyline down, to the benefit of no one. What the interviewer is hoping for in one way or another is entertainment. This can come in the sparks of disagreement or even genuine anger. Or it might be provided in the slow cringe of a guest's humiliation. To add spice to the mixture, there may well be a protagonist, carefully selected for an ability to disagree with everything you say or represent.

Working against everyone—you, any other guests and the television presenter as well—is the tyranny of the clock. There is a slot to be filled; no more, no less. Therefore, you have to be very quick off the mark to say what you have come to say. Polite chat is out of the question. But so, oddly enough, is aggression. Though a good fight has a great deal of overall entertainment value, it is disastrous for you. Remember the odd alchemy that takes place during a television interview. The interviewer, no matter how slick and glamorous and professional he or she might be, is suddenly transmogrified. Through the magic of television (and magic it truly seems to be) the driver of the Clapham omnibus is talking to you directly. And as any London driver knows, aggression aimed at the person behind the wheel of a bus is aggression dangerously misdirected.

Fortunately, pure aggression is not really called for anyway. Because of technical limitations, only one person at a time can talk on television—the same holds true for radio and the telephone. More than one voice raised in simultaneous discussion, or worse still, dispute, results in indistinguishable cacophony and plays havoc in the control room. All interviewers know this. Now that you know it as well, you are in control.

If you do not like what is being said, break the habit of a lifetime and simply interrupt. The interviewer will immediately go quiet. But if at all possible, do it gently and with kindness because, in the final analysis, you are interrupting the driver of the Clapham omnibus as well.

If, on the other hand, you think you are just in your stride and getting your point across quite nicely when the interviewer himself interrupts, simply ignore him and plough on. He will soon give up. Mrs Thatcher's mastery of this technique was—and no doubt still is—without parallel, as this conclusion of an interview with Brian Walden (no slouch himself) attests:

Mrs Thatcher:	'. . . I held these passionate convictions . . . reasonably, firmly, strongly . . .'
Brian Walden:	'Prime Minister, I must . . .'
Mrs Thatcher:	'Britain, they knew what . . .'
Brian Walden:	'I must stop you there.'
Mrs Thatcher:	'No . . . no, you must not.'
Brian Walden:	'I must. Thank you very much indeed.'
Mrs Thatcher:	'Strong leadership will continue.'

As apparently will any interview until Mrs Thatcher says otherwise.

So long as you are in control, questions that do not help you put your point across—or even worse, might be embarrassing for you to answer—can be harmlessly deflected using any number of formula phrases (each of which, it should be noted, contains the second personal pronoun):

'The question you should be asking yourself is . . .'
'The point you should be addressing . . .'
'You must remember that . . .'
'You must look at the facts . . .'
'You can put that another way, you know . . .'

Labour Prime Minister Harold Wilson had a typically pragmatic and effective way of dealing with questions he did not choose to answer. He would begin by singling out the offensive query with praise: 'Good question, that. I'll come back to it. Meanwhile I'll tell you what happened in

Blackpool in 1924 . . .', and the hapless interviewer would suddenly be hearing a reminiscence about Ernest Bevan.

Enoch Powell, paradoxically one of the most intellectual and yet popular performers on television interviews, uses an even more effective change of tack when he dislikes a question. 'Put that question to so-and-so', he will say. 'And while you're at it, the question you should be asking is . . .' and then he will proceed to ask himself the precise question that he has come prepared to answer. He does this so skilfully that he does not appear to be evading anything. Rather, he is seen to be helping in arriving at some profound truth, reached only after taking us, his audience, through a mire of dangerous misinformation. Whatever your views on his politics, his is consistently a masterful performance.

On this particular front Mrs Thatcher, at least as Prime Miinister, was, alas, less effective. When asked a question she did not like—on rising unemployment figures, for example—she was apt to respond, 'Why do you ask me that? Why don't you refer to the success of union legislation and the creation of jobs and pride in this country?' The trouble with this approach is its combination of aggression and stridency. Any question of politics and policies apart, it is this sort of attack—which through the magic of the medium the poor viewer sees as personally directed—that probably accounted for the high degree of personal unpopularity from which Mrs Thatcher suffered when in office.

Her successor, while hardly a premier television performer, has avoided that animosity. On television, he is a man given to curiously blended clichés ('I'm not going to beat my chest, while painting myself into a corner', he confided to Sue Lawley during his first important, if not exactly in-depth, interview), weird circumlocutions and oddly Dickensian interjections of 'O yes, O yes'. Nevertheless, he is never threatening or hectoring on screen. That alone could account for the high level of personal popularity he enjoys when compared with the previous occupant of Number 10.

Baiting apart, another favourite trick of interviewers is to subject their guests to multiple questions. These questions—almost as confusing to the viewer as they are to the interview subject—are a potential minefield. They have often been carefully designed so that some parts of the question are negative, while others are positive. Do not even attempt to respond to the whole range of questions. Even if you could remember all of them—which is highly unlikely—your audience will not. Instead, calmly point out to the interviewer (and not incidentally to the viewers as well) that you have been asked a wide range of questions. Say you will try to tackle them individually. If one of the questions appeals to you, answer it, by all means. But if none of them does, ignore them. Just revert to the previous tactic and put across one of the statements you have prepared.

What should you do if your inquisitor starts to make adverse comments about your organization and its activities? As you already know, you must not let such remarks go by default. Defending them outright, however, is altogether too predictable. 'He would say that, wouldn't he?' is a phrase coined by Mandy Rice-Davies during the Profumo scandal in the 1960s. Its power is undimmed 30 years later.

In any case, some of the accusations hurled at you could well be precisely on target. No company is perfect, after all. If that should happen, do not even attempt to refute the charge directly. The television camera will invariably catch you out if you try. Instead of a head-on confrontation with the truth, attack the insulting question obliquely. Simply say to your inquisitor:

'If you believe that, you should come and see for yourself.'

By inviting the interviewer (who would not dream of taking up your invitation) you are, of course, simultaneously inviting the viewer. The driver of the Clapham omnibus (yet again) is even less likely to show up at your factory gates than your video adversary, but having been invited he or she is suddenly confident that your premises must be beyond reproach.

This is, on the face of it, an absurd line of reasoning. Yet, absurdly, it works. And on deeper analysis, why shouldn't it? After all, it is carefully couched in the kind of everyday language the Clapham driver uses, not the complicated prose that posh people tend to use to hoodwink other people. By keeping your language to that level, you are also speaking to all the old age pensioners and the children of school age and under who are listening with half an ear, if that. To leave them out when you are broadcasting is to sacrifice an important and influential part of any audience.

There is another important concept to remember: the interview is yours to do with what you will. After all, consider the language used to describe the situation you are in. *You* were asked if *you* would *grant* an interview. The medium came to you as a supplicant. It was entirely in your power to refuse. Graciously, however, you acceded. But that does not mean you need lose control. They—meaning the researchers, the producer, the interviewer—are merely arranging the details. Why then, should you follow their lead by responding to questions that their staff have planned to lead you into a journalistic elephant trap?

No. You are the expert. You are responsible for the product or activity that aroused television interest in the first place. You know much more than your interviewer why things are done the way they are. Therefore, you owe it to yourself, and to the organization you are being paid to represent, to be positive and in control. On top of everything else, it is your responsibility to repolarize the direction your interview is taking if you think there is a risk of failing to get your predetermined points across.

BBC producer Stephen Hyland aptly likened a television interview to a high dive:

> You get yourself up on the diving board and every question you are asked is an opportunity for you to dive in whichever end of the pool you want to go and execute any kind of dive that you want: Headers, flip flops, somersaults, back flips, belly flops, whatever. You decide which dive and which direction you want to go to and don't be led by the interviewer unless of course he's going where you want to go.

Perhaps, on reflection, bellyflops are to be avoided. Nevertheless, the essence of Hyland's metaphor retains its truth. For all the paraphernalia and panoply that might surround you in the studio, the effectiveness of television is based on one thing: the opportunity to address someone on the subject of your choice in the intimacy of that person's own living room, sitting room, drawing room, lounge, kitchen, family room, bed-sit or even bathroom.

To reach that person effectively you need do only three things:

- Capture his or her attention.

- Retain the viewer's interest.
- Leave a lasting impression.

To succeed in getting your own point across, there are only three more rules to obey:

- Decide what you want to say. Then go there and say it.
- Let nothing go by default.
- Stay off other people's business.

It is simplicity itself. With this foreknowledge, you are suddenly transformed from a potential television victim into a cool, calm and confident master of the medium.

You have tamed the video lion. But what happens when the lion holds sway? It is not that rare an occurrence, as even a relatively infrequent television viewer can attest. No matter how often it happens, however, it is always fascinating—if discomforting—to watch.

Bob Newhart, the popular American television writer and performer realized this when he introduced such a sequence into an episode of his long-running situation comedy, in which he starred as a prominent Chicago psychologist.

Dr Hartley, as the character is called, has been asked to appear on a live early-morning TV chat show. He is flattered by this unexpected request (his name had been put forward by a friend). Therefore, without giving the matter much thought—and without knowing anything about the show on which he has been invited to appear—he accepts the invitation, at least in part because the glamorous blonde programme presenter who issues the invitation is so appealing.

Later, when asked by his wife what on earth he plans to do on the show, his response is airily vague. 'Oh, I'll talk about the overall effectiveness of group therapy', he says with confidence.

As the night wears on, that confidence begins to erode a bit. In the dark hours before dawn, pre-show butterflies first start fluttering in his stomach. He is at last beginning to realize the significance of what he has agreed to. 'I wonder what she's going to ask me', he muses. But instead of subjecting himself to the discipline of anticipating the questions he can expect, he dismisses his qualms.

By the next morning, his earlier confidence has returned, reinforced by the programme presenter's warm greeting and somewhat touching alarm at questioning a man so eminent in his complex speciality.

On the set, but before the cameras begin to roll, she remarks on his calm demeanour:

> 'I'm glad *you're* relaxed. You know, I'm a little nervous, myself. I've never interviewed a psychologist . . . If I start to ramble a little, or if I get into an area I'm not conversant in, you'll help me out, won't you?'

Dr Hartley, ever the gentleman, reassures her:

> 'Don't worry about it. If you get in trouble, just turn it over to me, and I'll wing it.'

The floor manager then gives the countdown and suddenly they are on the air:

> 'My first guest is psychologist Robert Hartley. It's been said that today's psychologist is nothing more than a conman, a snake oil salesman, flimflamming innocent people, peddling cures for everything from nailbiting to a lousy lovelife . . . And I agree. We'll ask Dr Hartley to defend himself after this message.'

With a furrowing of his brows and a few sidelong glances, Dr Hartley incredulously asks his inquisitor:

> 'Was that on the air?'

Once again, the programme presenter is friendliness itself:

> 'Oh, that was just what we call a "grabber". You know, it keeps the audience from tuning out.'

Seeking some further reassurance, he asks:

> 'We won't be doing any more grabbing, will we?'

> 'Oh no. From now on we'll just *talk*', she gushes.

After another brief countdown, the cameras turn again, and so does the face of the interviewer:

'Dr Hartley, according to a recently published survey, the average fee for a private session with a psychologist is $40.'

'That's about right.'

'*Right?* I don't think it's *right*. What other practitioner gets $40 an hour?'

Looking like a rabbit caught in the headlamps of an on-coming lorry, the poor trapped psychologist tries to inject some humour into the grim proceedings:

'My plumber,' he rather tentatively suggests.

Yet the blonde juggernaut will not be diverted by a joke:

'Plumbers guarantee their work. Do *you?*'

Dr Hartley is now genuinely confused:

'Gee . . . I don't understand . . . Why all of a sudden? . . .'

The interviewer is relentless:

'I asked you if you guaranteed your work.'

Defensively, Dr Hartley replies:

'Well I can't guarantee that each and every person who walks through the door is going to be cured . . .'

'You mean you ask $40 an hour and you guarantee *nothing?*'

'I . . . I . . . I validate . . .', he interjects in a conciliatory tone.

'Is that your answer?' she persists.

By now, beginning to be really worried, Dr Hartley leans across and whispers behind his hand:

'Could I have a word with you in private?'

'Chicago is waiting for your answer,' she declaims.

'Well . . . uh . . . Chicago . . . everyone who comes in doesn't pay $40 an hour . . .'

'Do you *ever* cure *anybody?*' she interrupts.

'Well, I wouldn't say *cure* . . .'

'So your answer is "no".'

'No, my answer is not "no". I get results. Many of my patients solve their problems and go on to become successful . . .'

'Successful at *what?*'

'Professional athletes, clergymen, some go on to lead large corporations. One of my patients is an elected official . . .'

Seizing on that last revelation, she recoils and strikes:

'A what?'

'Er . . . nothing, nothing . . .,' he says, desperately trying to undo the mistake he has made.

'Did you say an elected official?'

'I might have . . . I forget.'

'Who is it?' she demands.

'Well, I can't divulge his identity.'

'Why?' she demands indignantly. 'There is a deranged man out there in a position of power!'

'He isn't deranged . . . anymore,' he adds meekly.

'But he was when he came to see you. And you said yourself you do not give guarantees . . .'

Suddenly, before he knows it, but none too soon, Dr Hartley's interview is at an end. The programme presenter goes on to announce:

'After this message we will meet our choice of woman of the year, Sister Mary Catherine . . .'

The cameras are off. And suddenly, the gorgon of the television studio once again becomes a warm and charming woman:

. . . 'Thank you, Dr Hartley. You were terrific. I mean I wish we had more time . . .'

For the first time, yet too late, Dr Hartley finds the courage to interrupt firmly:

'We had plenty.'

'I really enjoyed it,' she insists.

'You would have enjoyed Pearl Harbor,' he retorts.

At this point, Sister Mary Catherine, an angelic veiled figure, is ushered to her seat on the soundstage. The gracious programme presenter enthuses:

'Good morning, Sister, it's wonderful of you to come at this hour.'

Dr Hartley, removing his microphone, leaves with a word of advice to the next guest:

'If I were you, I wouldn't get into religion. She'll chew your legs off.'

Unfortunately, the nightmare does not end there for Dr Hartley. As would be the case in real life, a television interview that goes so woefully wrong can be the springboard for a good deal more media attention. After all, he had inadvertently revealed that a former patient of his was an elected official. With a revelation such as that, a vicious but not terribly interesting feature interview suddenly becomes hot news.

The interview segment itself is repeated on the next news bulletin. And there follows a barrage of calls for further interviews from competitor television broadcasters, radio stations and important newspapers.

Of course, Bob Newhart's script is meant to be funny. And it is. But it carries several cautionary truths in its humour that are worth examining, since they typify all that can go wrong in television for the unwary, the unsuspecting, the untrained. Therefore, it is worth dissecting exactly what went wrong in what should have been a harmless couple of minutes of television chat about the virtues of group therapy.

Dr Hartley's first mistake was to give in to his ego. Being approached out of the blue by a well-known television presenter (well known at least to everyone but him—he had neither known of her nor seen her programme) is naturally a boost to self-esteem. But that is no excuse for acquiescing to an interview. What Dr Hartley should have done first was look into the background of the programme and its presenter. He should have quizzed his colleagues and family for their opinions.

Why do *they* watch the programme? Because it is intelligently informative? Or perhaps the programme's popularity is based on the savagery of its hostess. Either could be the case. Best of all would be a deferment of decision until he himself had had the opportunity to see several editions of the chat show. Then, and only then, should he even have considered going on.

But as you have seen, even that is not enough information to go on. He should have asked exactly what points the presenter wanted to cover. Why? What precipitated her interest in the topic: had there been any recent books, articles or surveys that would make his appearance desirably timely from the programme's point of view? If so, he would have to know before appearing or even agreeing to appear. As it happened, he was alone on the programme. But what if someone else had been scheduled to appear with him. Who would that be? With what point of view? And with what credentials?

Then, Dr Hartley should have asked himself why—ego apart—he might want to be on television. Did he have anything specific to say? What advantage would he gain from the exposure? What could he lose? Conversely, what risks, if any, would there be in refusing to appear? He should have weighed these two points to determine which came out in his favour.

Assuming that, after that exercise, the benefits of television outweighed the potential drawbacks, Dr Hartley should then have tried to second-guess the presenter in her choice—or more probably her researcher's choice—of questions. True, he did ask himself one question, but that was as far as it went. As you have already seen, the list could run on for page after page. But unless and until each of those questions could have been answered or deflected to his satisfaction, Dr Hartley should not have appeared before the cameras.

When fully prepared for what might go wrong, he should then have decided what would go right. What two or three points did he want to get across to the few million or so people who might be watching a popular early-morning Chicago chat show? And how, using what analogies, what homilies, what popular forms of language would he deliver those nuggets of information that he was putting at risk his professional and personal reputation to convey? A bland and general desire to convey the virtues of group therapy was no substitute for careful analysis of what his message to the audience should be.

Once in the studio, Dr Hartley continued, for the most part, to get things disastrously, if comically, wrong. Admittedly, he did accept the unfamiliar ordeal of professional television make-up. But his performance went downhill from there.

His chat with the programme presenter was akin to waving a red rag at a bull. Over-confidence to the point of condescension can only stimulate an aggressive interviewer to dangerous excess. That, in fact, is what took place. But even having made that dangerous error, the hapless Dr Hartley could have still salvaged a bad situation.

Once the cameras started, the television presenter's attack was immediate. At the first mention of the word 'conman' every alarm in Dr Hartley's being should have sounded. With proper determination, he could have stopped his inquisitor from getting beyond that point with a well-timed interruption of controlled indignation. Instead, he let everything she said go by default, allowing her aspersions to stick.

Yet even then all was not lost. After the break, Dr Hartley had a chance to recover the situation. The interviewer's tactic of diving right into the cost of psychotherapy was a foolish one. At this point, her victim could have turned the tables quite easily. When the programme presenter first brought up the subject of cost, these were her exact words:

> 'Dr Hartley, according to a recently published survey, the average fee for a private session with a psychologist is $40.'

Here, Dr Hartley could well have broken in with words along these lines:

> 'When you reach a point in your life when you need someone to talk to, someone you know who has benefited from years of professional training on how best to listen to you, your first consideration isn't cost.'

If the interviewer then—foolishly, at this point—had persisted with the question of the $40 fee, Dr Hartley could have interrupted again:

'You go on about that $40. But what else would you spend that $40 on? Dinner in a restaurant? A new hat? A gadget for the kitchen? For what you might spend on one of those, you could be well on the way to achieving serenity or peace of mind. And those are things you can't put a price on.'

Some of Dr Hartley's other mistakes are obvious. His retort about the plumber, for instance, was not a bad joke in itself, but it was glib. As such, it gave his interviewer an irresistible urge to turn to righteous indignation. As for his unwitting revelation about the elected official on his patient roll, that was the result of allowing himself to be cornered. To defend himself on a lesser point—the type of person who would seek his services—he sacrificed his integrity on a much greater point.

However, none of this would have arisen had Dr Hartley stuck to his first intention: to talk about the benefits of group therapy. Admittedly, his interviewer was not exactly forthcoming with a cue for that particular topic. She obviously had her own axe to grind—preferably against Dr Hartley's skull. Nevertheless, with determination, he could have turned one of her questions or statements to his own advantage and so brought the subject up himself. For instance, when rather unfairly asked if he ever cured anybody, Dr Hartley could legitimately, and forcefully, have interjected:

'When you're a psychologist you don't cure anyone. You help your patients to cure themselves. And one of the most effective ways of doing that is by getting a group of patients together to talk through their own fears and problems. This is known as group therapy. When you're a member of such a group you suddenly find that you're not alone in your worries and confusion. You have support. You have people you can talk to freely, without inhibition. You find you can build on one another's strengths. At the same time, you develop new understanding of your own problems. As psychologist in charge of such a group, you merely guide the group on their own path to awareness . . .'

. . . Or words to that effect. No interviewer would dare interrupt such a confident discourse.

But of course Dr Hartley did not do any of those things that he should have done. Therefore, he paid the consequences. Shocked by his indiscretion, his patients descended *en masse* and demanded that their files be turned over to them immediately. His colleagues gave him a month to leave his consulting rooms. Even his wife, who quite properly had no idea of the existence of the elected official who had been a patient, made it her mission in life to discover the politician's identity.

In effect, the hero's career, his self-esteem and even his home life were ruined by a television segment barely two minutes in length. Who was to blame? Not the interviewer. She was merely doing her job of providing entertainment with a bit of information thrown in. No. It was Dr Hartley himself, guilty on two counts of television crime. First, he failed to appreciate the significance of any time spent before a television camera. Secondly, he underestimated the skills needed to turn a television interview to his own advantage.

The punishment for those crimes is both immediate and long-lasting to self-esteem and professional standing. Worse still, there is no parole.

12
Playing host to the TV beast

It is one thing to expose yourself to the rigours of a television interview in a studio. It is quite another to let down the barriers of instinctive territoriality and allow a video interview to take place on your own turf. Under no circumstances is it a decision to be taken lightly, whether the venue is to be your office or your home. The perils of the wandering crew and the conflicting demands of hospitality versus expedience are highlighted in this chapter.

Thanks to highly sophisticated developments in video technology, television is no longer the studio-bound medium of its infancy. Today, when something of interest is happening anywhere in the world, the audience expects its television representatives to be there on the spot, reporting the news as and where it happens. That is a welcome development for armchair travellers; perhaps less welcome for you, if your office happens to be where what seems to be a major story just happens to be breaking.

Having discovered how to tame the video beast on its own territory, you must now bear in mind certain rules for controlling the creature on your ground. First of all, forget any of the conventions of hospitality. Though you might have been taught from your earliest years that a host's duty to guests is inviolate, the presence of a television camera and its human hangers-on makes such strictures obsolete, not to say downright dangerous.

Begin by asking yourself why the interviewer, camera and crew are all going to the trouble and inconvenience of darkening your door rather than asking you to the studio. The reason could be innocence itself: a change of scene on television is as welcome as anywhere else, and probably more so, since the medium is so visual. Perhaps the director simply feels that your interview would be more colourful in your own environment.

The director might well be right, but that is hardly your primary concern. After all, what is the definition of local colour under these circumstances? While offices are not, in themselves, terribly interesting places, they can be dangerously revealing venues, particularly when seen through the lens of a skilled professional. The apparently innocuous picture on your wall, the jokey plaything on your desktop or—perish the thought—the mildly naughty calendar behind your chair can all be used to undercut your message and destroy your credibility.

This holds especially true in an emergency, as P&O was to learn in the immediate aftermath to the sinking of the *Herald of Free Enterprise* in Zeebrugge harbour. As soon as word of the disaster broke, a video crew raced to the London offices of Townsend Thoreson, operators of the vessel, which had been acquired by P&O European Ferries only weeks before.

The disaster occurred after office hours and, understandably, only two public affairs staff happened to be on hand. Whether or not it was their decision to admit a television news crew was never made clear. However, the result was irretrievably damning. Since the hapless P&O PROs were, like most of the rest of the world, uninformed about either the cause or extent of the crisis, the camera reverted to the ever-popular fly-on-the-wall technique. It showed the poor, unprepared pair hopelessly swamped with telephone enquiries. At one point, the camera lovingly dwelt on the pen in the hand of one of them. The viewer then saw that, instead of taking notes, the man charged with crisis response was doodling on the front page of a well-thumbed daily tabloid newspaper. A slow pan then revealed the office walls, unsurprisingly hung with ranges of glossy holiday brochures promising glamorous, trouble-free crossings on Townsend Thoreson vessels. To underline the sudden irony these leaflets assumed under tragic circumstances, the television reporter then referred to them as 'hanging limply' in the aftermath of the disaster. The fact is, of course, they merely hung there as they had first been put up. They did not suddenly go limp with shame after the incident. Nevertheless, that is how the viewer remembered seeing them after their limpness had been highlighted by the commentator. Then, going in for the kill, she went on to intone lugubriously: 'Wherever the *Herald of Free Enterprise* emergency is being controlled, it's certainly not from here.' Journalistic contempt emanated from her entire being. The audience, inevitably, came to share in the horror and indignation.

A hatchet job? Perhaps, but who can really blame the reporter? She was told to go to Townsend Thoreson's offices and produce a story. Though the shipping company was unprepared, it was sufficiently cooperative (or naïve) to allow the camera crew on the premises. The journalist was under pressure. When a journalist is under pressure, the only thing to do is transfer that pressure to the subject of the story. After all, the poor woman had to do something to fill air time. And so she did, quite effectively. In fact, so effective was the post-sinking coverage of the *Herald of Free Enterprise* that the name Townsend Thoreson almost immediately disappeared from the world's shipping lanes. Forever.

Fortunately, there are ways to avoid a similar fate to your corporate identity in the wake of a visitation by the media to your premises. Begin by ensuring that you have an effective security operation in force at all entrances. This does not mean a squad of Neanderthal heavies ready to pounce on any journalist with the temerity to arrive on your doorstep uninvited or unannounced. Instead, your first line of defence should be an effective electronic security system operated by a team of well-groomed, impeccably polite and thoroughly briefed security people. It should be their job to deal cordially but nevertheless firmly with any unexpected media doorsteppers.

Clear instructions should tell these guardians of your office sanctity whom to contact—together with a full list of alternatives—if and when reporters arrive unexpectedly during the course of normal business activities or during an emergency. (If reporters arrive unexpectedly, you can bet there is an emergency on somewhere in your organization, whether you know it or not.)

Now, the question is whether to talk or not to talk. If you do know what is going on, the cause behind the visit, so much the better. If not, find out quickly, either through your own organization or by agreeing to meet—informally and off the record and nowhere within sight of any cameras—a single representative of the media invasion in as neutral and bland a room as possible, as close as possible to the foyer where the reporters are being held. Too much can be learnt by a lengthy peregrination through the corridors of commerce.

Deciding on the spur of the moment whether or not to submit to a television interview is certainly not easy. Therefore, do not be tempted to give a quick response, either positive or negative. After all, you owe nothing to the television crew that showed up on your doorstep uninvited and unannounced. Instead, listen to what they have to say, then escort them back to your secure area and ask them to wait there for as quick a response as you can reasonably manage.

At this point they will moan about the deadline to which they are working; the broadcast slot they have reserved for this particular news item; and the difficulty of starting afresh. Nod sagely, look sympathetic and ignore their demands for an immediate response. The decision will be yours, not theirs.

If, in a reasonable amount of time, you can assemble your thoughts, decide on a suitable location and—most important of all—come up with the requisite statements or messages, give in to the request. If, on the other hand, you are likely to lose more than you will gain by a television appearance, reject the proposal. But do it politely. Tell them you simply do not have the time at the moment. Ask them to consider postponing the particular story and setting an appointment for some time in the future. They will not agree, but at least you look cooperative.

Finally, if you turn the crew down, reconcile yourself to the fact that your unwelcome and unexpected visitors will proceed to set up their lights and cameras in as obtrusive a place as possible—either in your foyer or just outside your building—and attempt to cobble together a video clip in any case. Your refusal to talk to them will be noted, but depending on how diplomatically you handle the situation, any damage could be limited. If you are lucky, 'unavailable for comment' might well be the only mud slung your way.

Of course, television crews are not always unexpected—let alone unwelcome—guests. There are times when you might actively cooperate with a suggestion for on-site televising, or even suggest it yourself. There are, however, dangers in these scenarios as well.

First, there is a tendency to be altogether too cooperative. After all, these people have come all this way to talk to you—perhaps even at your instigation. Surely, you might think, it is your responsibility to make them feel welcome; to show them the same warm courtesy you would accord any welcome or at least influential guest to your premises.

Resist that temptation.

Tell a television reporter and crew to feel at home and they will do just that. For them, it is more than a figure of speech. It is an open invitation to more disruption, more disorganization, more disarray than you would ever have dreamed possible.

A television crew unleashed on your office is like a whirlwind. Within minutes you will find window blinds torn open, furniture rearranged, pot plants ripped apart and your mainframe computer terminals torn from their sockets to be replaced by a sinister tangle of thick black cables.

However, any such damage is superficial. The real danger of a video crew unleashed is the havoc they will wreak on your records. After all, on their own territory they have no qualms about leafing the files. You have told them to make themselves at home. The same rules—or lack of them—apply. And from the video crew's point of view, all sorts of interesting and useful things could turn up in your desk drawers. Such material could give a much more interesting angle to the story the interviewer is already contemplating.

To avoid this nightmare of invasion and violation, set the ground rules from the start and assign at least one member of staff to the crew full time while they are in attendance. That person should, of course, be well briefed beforehand to be polite, ostensibly cooperative and totally discreet. Professed (if not actual) ignorance of the topics to be covered in the interview is a distinct advantage in your minder-designate. So is an inability to be embarrassed by such tasks as accompanying the visitors on any and all missions beyond the interview room—even to the lavatory and back. The effective minder can know no shame.

Meanwhile, you—the flower, the media honeypot—who attracted this video swarm in the first place, must keep your distance. By all means welcome them on their arrival, but then hand them over to the minder (or minders) you selected in advance and then withdraw, arranging to meet the crew at the room you have already chosen to put at their disposal for the interview.

A word about this room: your office would do. After all, you feel comfortable there, and its paraphernalia probably says a great deal about who you are and what you do. But there is always the distinct possibility that it might say too much. Obviously, confidential sales charts, profit projections and the like should come down. So should any work in progress such as advertising roughs or product designs. Go beyond such material, however, and put on your cloak of empathy. How would your office look to a television audience? Try to anticipate what shots might be set up: you behind the desk; a cosy chat on the sofa; standing at your window overlooking what? Look at your office with fresh eye before committing yourself to its use for the interview.

If, after that examination, you do opt for your office as the right setting, make any necessary changes and then prepare to vacate the room entirely until the appointed hour of the interview itself. Forget the disruption to your work routine that this might cause; that is the inevitable drawback of the office interview.

In any case, no matter what location you decide is best, make yourself scarce. By absenting yourself in this way, you eliminate the irresistible temptation of the host or hostess to jolly your 'guests' along in their efforts. This, of course, would mean endless chatting. From your experience of studio interviews, you know the dangers to which that can lead: give away too much before an interview and you lose control of the situation. If you are not around, you cannot give anything away.

When, at the appointed hour, you arrive at that designated room, you will most likely find it unrecognizable. Do not be put off. Simply position yourself where the interviewer asks and proceed exactly as you would do in a more conventional studio environment. Whether you go to television or television comes to you, your responsibilities and the techniques used to carry out those responsibilities are unchanged. Make your statements or messages at all costs, let nothing go by default and keep off other people's business.

Though you might be interviewed in the comfortable, even cosy confines of your own office, those people who are temporarily sharing the room with you are not your guests. You owe them nothing but basic courtesy. Certainly, they feel they owe you nothing at all—not even gratitude for letting them into your sanctum. For the sake of a good (meaning juicy) interview, they would happily flay you alive with your own executive letter knife. Remember that. It will help you to keep the requisite sense of distance emotionally, intellectually and socially. Then all should go well.

But once the interview is over, do not relax. If anything, become more vigilant. Increase that sense of polite separation. As long as the crew is on your premises—and you share it with them—you are still fair game. On that understanding, remove yourself entirely. Lie. Say you have an unmissable appointment scheduled for 10 minutes after the interview is due to finish. If necessary, get in your car and drive away. Go and play squash. Go and have a drink. Go home. Go anywhere, but do it quickly. The longer you stay behind, the more likely your sense of relief will betray you into telling the crew something they need not or even should not know.

Only when you know for certain that the coast is clear should you attempt to return. Overall, the experience of an interview on your own premises is one of dispossession. While television is in residence, your office, in effect, becomes theirs. This holds true even if you own the entire building. In a sense, a visit from a television crew has become the late twentieth century equivalent of an Elizabethan royal progress in which by custom the monarch, though strictly speaking merely a guest, became the official hostess. Similarly, if you have the temerity to play host to a video crew, you should have the wisdom to surrender temporary sovereignty of your own premises. No matter what you do, television will have the last word.

13
You have a story to tell

Devoted to a brief look at effective narrative techniques. Communication is, after all, a skill. A few people are born with it. Most have to acquire it. Few do. This becomes readily apparent in a crisis, when a senior executive, usually a confident and decisive individual, stumbles through a press conference, an interview or even an employee forum. Those few who do succeed in getting their messages across use a few time-honoured techniques and a fundamental understanding of what makes people sit up and take notice. These are presented here.

Television is often maligned as little more than an idiot box. This is hardly surprising. It is part of human nature to denigrate that which seems to hold a mysterious power over us, that which we might even quietly fear.

Nevertheless, some of the least likely subjects have made successful television series. Who, for instance, might have predicted long-term success for a television programme devoted to astronomy? Surely, so complex a subject, with its mind-boggling, literally cosmic concepts, esoteric vocabulary and lack of any obvious action is above and beyond the level of the typical television viewer.

Not necessarily, as Patrick Moore and his ever-popular *The Sky at Night* was to prove.

The same holds true for any number of highly unlikely television success stories. The tweedy Barbara Woodhouse, for example, was hardly the sort of person whose photograph you would choose from a casting album as someone destined for television stardom. Nor was her speciality topic—dog training—of particularly riveting interest to most of the population. Similarly, David Bellamy, with his rough and tumble Latin pronunciations of complex botanical nomenclature, has opened up the world of plants to millions. Miriam Stoppard has even gone so far as to break down the final Western television taboo: she brings the topic of death by any number of dread diseases to a fascinated teatime audience.

Like Percy Thrower, whose praises were sung in an earlier chapter, each of these diverse and sometimes even idiosyncratic television personalities has something in common. No matter what the complexity of their topics, each manages to convey his or her subject in a manner readily understood by a mass audience.

The driver of the Clapham omnibus is not usually given to the more arcane principles of plant propagation. Neither he nor she is generally thrilled by the behaviour of an obscure supernova. The driver is not likely to want to train a gun dog. And as for cancer, it is not a subject to dwell upon, thank you very much.

What, then, accounts for the television success of all these unlikely candidates for stardom? For one, they themselves are enthused by their subjects. This enthusiasm comes across in the liveliness of their presentation. But, of course, that is not the sole reason for their success.

Not one of these highly popular television personalities is produced from the usual mould of television personalities. Instead they are—or at least seem to be—true to themselves. In appearance, they maintain a degree of eccentricity or at least highly personal style. Their manner of speaking encompasses a number of highly diverse accents according to class and region: Oxbridge academic, Home Counties tennis club, North London, East End. Some even have distinct speech impediments which, in theory, should disqualify them for television success.

Nevertheless, they are all stars of greater or lesser magnitude. The reason for their success can be found in the way in which they tell their stories. They recognize—probably instinctively—the intellectual limitations of the mass audience they are being paid princely sums to reach. Instead of condescending from this point of recognition, they revel in the discipline that those limitations demand. They manage to filter highly complex material through their minds to save the essential truths and eliminate the extraneous details that would make their material otherwise unapproachable for most of the television audience.

You can and should do the same.

Begin by forgetting what you are. Though Miriam Stoppard is no doubt an expert physician, she does not present herself as such. Naturally, she relies on her professional background for her knowledgeable treatment of the medical subjects she covers on television. However, her media persona is hardly that of the typical GP, who retreats into esoterica to maintain a comfortable distance between self and patient. Instead, Dr Stoppard comes across as the kindly woman next door—better educated, no doubt, but at the same time warm, human and, above all, concerned. You could go to her with any problem, whether it is to borrow a cup of detergent or to ask about a disturbing lump that has suddenly appeared in your breast. In other words, she sacrifices most, if not quite all, of her professional dignity for a more worthy cause: the effective communication of her message. That is one of the secrets of her televisual effectiveness.

Why, then, should you do any differently? Being a business executive is certainly neither more grand nor more worthy than being a physician. Consequently, you should have no qualms in shedding that executive carapace when you have the opportunity to appear on television. After all, simply as a human being there is—or should be—considerably more to you than your job title. When you hold forth at home or at a friend's house or in the changing room at your squash club, it is not the assistant vice president in charge of marketing who is talking. It is you. Similarly, it is you, a fully rounded individual, who should be telling your story on television, using the language you would use not to your peers at work but to your family and friends.

This is not always easy. For instance, in the course of training policemen and women (several thousand during the past decade) a frequently voiced objection was 'If I talked as you say, they would laugh me out of the police station.' It is a legitimate worry, but one that should be put into perspective: in the United Kingdom there are just over 100 000 members of the police, most of whom are on duty and not watching television at any given time. On the other hand, there is a population of more than 50 million, of whom a substantial portion are virtually always watching television. Who is it more important to get through to?

In any case, when you appear on television you need never worry about over-simplifying matters for your peers back at the office or police station or stock market or wherever. Instead, see yourself as a messenger.

It is your mission to explain your point of view and that of your organization to those who know not and care not but who, nevertheless, will be so taken by the skilful way in which you impart your message that they listen and take note almost in spite of themselves.

As you already know, the basic technique is simplicity itself:

- You attract their attention by using the second personal pronoun.
- You sustain their interest by being interesting and giving examples.
- You describe things visually and pictorially to leave your audience with lasting images to remember.

But there are other factors of effective story-telling on television to bear in mind as well.

As the division of labour accelerates, people increasingly specialize in more and more arcane areas of expertise. Each profession, every sector within that profession, and every company within a given sector therefore tends to evolve its own sublanguage, going beyond the purely technical demands of more traditional jargon. This can also be seen in central government and local government bureaucracies. The end result of this division of labour is a marked and increased divergence from the language the rest of the nation speaks when it is at home.

In itself, there is nothing wrong with this trend. As long as people within a group understand one another, they can communicate effectively. Of course, by their coldly restrictive and/or technical natures, sublanguages tend to lose many of the more endearing aspects of everyday speech: sympathy, imagination and humour all too often fall by the wayside. The main trouble with this verbal shorthand is that it frequently degenerates into an intellectual shortcut as well. As the reasoning becomes foreshortened, so does truth. Eventually, there is the danger that the poverty of the sublanguage itself comes to influence the quality of thought it is meant to express.

Sometimes, this becomes apparent only when it becomes necessary for a speaker of this language to communicate effectively with outsiders. More often than not, the speaker has become so immured in the use of the sublanguage to describe the organization that spawned it, that he or she finds it difficult to describe that organization in any other terms.

Instead, at the prospect of opening their closed world to others, insiders seek emotional refuge in their by-now probably incomprehensible lingo. For an outsider, this can seem very close to pomposity.

It is not a new phenomenon. Forty years ago that leading exponent of clear English, George Orwell, sought to diagnose and dissect the disorder of verbal pomposity. He wrote:

> The English language becomes ugly and inaccurate because our thoughts are foolish, but the slovenliness of our language makes it easier for us to have foolish thoughts.

Though perhaps we can afford to be slovenly and slipshod among our immediate peers (who might just understand what we are getting at anyway), it is a grievous mistake to make this assumption for outsiders.

Nevertheless, this is what all too many experts tend to do on television. Using their debased sublanguage both to mould their own thoughts as well as to communicate to outsiders, they actually lose track of what it is they are really saying. Astonishingly, this does not bother them. Their use of the sublanguage has become so habitual that it no longer seems necessary to believe what they are thinking or saying. Admittedly, some may indulge in this motiveless subterfuge more skilfully than others during a broadcast, but any subsequent transcript or video tape always reveals the degree of nonsense spoken. It also highlights the peculiar style that any language composed of jargon and half truths inevitably assumes. Among business executives and government officials, the characteristics of this style are dead metaphors, empty pretensions and meaningless words and phrases. Or, as Orwell went on to say in his own inimitable style:

> As soon as certain topics are raised, the concrete melts into the abstract and no-one seems able to think of turns of phrase that are not hackneyed: prose consists less and less of words chosen for the sake of their meaning and more and more of phrases tacked together like the sections of a pre-fabricated hen-house.

An accomplished practitioner of this executive-speak can go on indefinitely. In fact, he or she often does. The effect on the audience is predictably hypnotic, usually causing no particular offence but winning no advantage, either. The driver of the Clapham omnibus will not have been asked to think and so remains apathetic to whatever point it is you might be trying—however feebly—to put across.

But what happens when you break yourself of that bad executive-speak habit, as indeed you must if you hope to succeed on television? A number of things occur almost simultaneously. As you would expect, the fluency and competence of your performance is raised instantly. But more important than that is what happens internally. Suddenly, when you stop speaking like an executive, you stop thinking like one. As you break the Orwellian mould of hackneyed phrases and empty expressions, you also shatter constraints on ideas and innovations. You gain a new sense of coherence and purpose in your job. At the same time, your view of the company you work for shifts for the better. When you can describe its function in clear, simple, concise language—as you have to do if you are addressing a child of 12 or the person behind the wheel of the ubiquitous Clapham omnibus—then the organization you represent is suddenly imbued with a new integrity or even legitimacy that you never before appreciated.

In good times, the ability to communicate on television in this way is certainly a bonus. In bad times it is nothing short of essential. Think back once again to all the disasters that television has covered in recent years: the aftermath of the plane explosion over Lockerbie, the Clapham Junction rail disaster, the capsizing of the *Herald of Free Enterprise* at Zeebrugge, the British Midland motorway crash, the blazing pyre of *Piper Alpha*, the oily wake of the *Exxon Valdez*, and the Gulf War. Each of these was of course horrific. And in each case television audiences were enabled to share at least a part of the horror, due to the timely and extensive coverage each of these events received on the national and international media.

The images of death and devastation will always stay with anyone who saw them. Almost equally long-lived will be the scorn that some of the companies and government agencies involved brought down upon themselves by their abysmal television performances in dealing with the crises. Why did they communicate so badly just when good communications were so important for everyone involved?

It is not as though they set out to leave an indelible stain on the collective consciousness of the viewing public. That would hardly be in their own interests. Instead, their sorry performance was the result of a retreat. No doubt unable to face the horror of the calamity with which they were forced to deal, they unwittingly withdrew behind the barriers of corporate language and corporate thought processes. There, they felt safe. It is an understandable thing for them to have done. Nevertheless, from a communications standpoint, it was lamentable.

What was the alternative?

A corporate disaster, by its very nature, is synonymous with a degree of chaos. With the best will in the world, and despite instantaneous electronic communications, no one person is at any one time fully in control of all the facts. Things keep changing. New information is always coming in, contradicting recent but suddenly unreliable reports. You never know when what you have been assured is solid fact will instantly turn into the wildest speculation. As a result, you are naturally guarded in what you have to say to the public. That is inevitable.

At the same time, you are being plagued by more journalists, radio reporters and television interviewers than you had ever contemplated in your worst media nightmares. All are clamouring for news—any news—about what has happened, what has caused the disaster to happen and what, if anything, your company is doing to deal with the emergency.

What do you do?

You revert to the single golden thread that has bound this slim volume together. You empathize. And you do it in several directions at once.

First, you put yourself in the place of the most important people of the moment: those individuals who are directly affected by the disaster at hand, be they friends, relatives, neighbours, or whoever. What do they know already? What do they need to know? How much of that need can you fulfil? And if you cannot give them full and immediate answers to their questions, how can you temporarily deflect those questions without causing undue concern?

Then, think about your secondary audience. What about your employees? How will they take this news? What bearing will it have on their jobs? On their futures? Depending on your company structure, what about shareholders, or partner companies, or parent companies? What about clients or users of your product? They all have genuine interests to greater or lesser degrees.

Then, of course, we come to the media themselves. They have time slots to fill, deadlines to meet. They need to know what? When? Where? Why? How much? How many? And they need to know it immediately. If they do not get the answers from you, they will get them from the plethora of would-be instant experts who creep out of the woodwork whenever a disaster occurs.

The needs of each of these categories of people require immediate attention. Naturally, the first priority in any company when an emergency occurs is to deal with the emergency itself. Yet the aftermath of a badly communicated emergency can prove to be an even more painful ordeal than the disaster that precipitated it. You have only to recall the cases of Union Carbide after Bhopal and Exxon after the *Valdez* to bring that point home.

Therefore, every company that has the potential for anything to go seriously wrong—which is the same as saying every single company or organization—should have a team whose dedicated job is to compile the information about that emergency for use by the outside world. Their work is akin to the illustrative list in Chapter 8.

Based on that list, and having reduced what you want to say to two or three fundamental messages, go on to determine the language you will use. Remember, you are no longer a business executive talking to other business executives. You are a thoughtful, compassionate, clear-headed human being addressing another single individual of your species (multiplied, of course, by several million) in as simple and direct and memorable a way as you know how. First, you must get that individual's attention. Then you must retain it. Then you must leave a lasting message behind.

The idea of *communication*, when it is isolated as a specialist skill, is inevitably a daunting prospect, especially televisual communication. After all, look at all those highly successful, very highly paid professionals who make so glamorous a living doing it.

Yet, as you will have learnt by now, the essence of any effective communication, and particularly communication on television, is simplicity itself. If you are doing it properly, nothing should be more natural. You are not standing up and addressing an auditorium full of people. Nor are you speaking in front of a camera before a faceless, potentially hostile mass of humanity.

No.

You are merely getting across a simple idea to a single 12-year-old child or that ever-receptive driver of a public conveyance that serves an inner suburb in southwest London. You begin by addressing him or her with a single word:

YOU

And the rest should, by now, come naturally.

Index

Acronyms, 71
Acting, professional, 12, 27-28
Active voice, 71
Adie, Kate, 103
Adrenalin, 24, 29, 96
Advertising:
 messages, 2-3, 70
 revenue, 59, 111
Aggression, unsuited to television interview, 117, 119
Aim, of communication event, 13
Alcohol, and interviews, 98-99
Anecdotes, use of, 72
Angle, of story, 38, 93
Appearance, while on television, 101-108
Attention:
 to attract, 26, 64-69
 to retain, 69-72
Audience composition, 25, 60-61, 69-70
Audience, television, 60-62, 68-72, 120
 size of, 60, 63, 68
Audiences, hostile, 30
Audio level, 101
Audio press release, 50-51

Bad news, attraction of, 90, 113-114
BBC, 47, 111-112
 rules for interviewing, 95
Behaviour, to suit situation, 10
Body language, 13, 29, 107

Brevity, 20
Broadsheets, 37

Cameraman, 100
Candour, best for television interview, 79
Checklist, for effective memos, 18-19
Children, power of persuasion, 70
Clarity, 20, 23-24
Cliché, 74, 75
Close-up, 79
Clothes, choice of, for television, 104-107
Cogency, 20
Collusion, 99
Commercial radio, 47-48
 station, how to approach, 50-52
Communication, 32, 63, 65, 145
Company journal, 23
Computer-generated copy, 18
Confrontation, 93-95
Control, of interview, 117, 118, 121
Control room, 101
Conventions, of letter writing, 20
Conversational style, for television, 67-69, 70
Credibility:
 among employees, 23-24
 on television, 56, 132
Critical faculty, 3, 4, 6, 8
 analysing a speaker, 5
Cynicism, about the press, 89

147

Delayed response, *see* Response, delayed
Deportment, 107
Detachment, a useful skill, 9, 13
Dictation, 17
Director, 101
Disasters, corporate, 81, 113, 143–145
Disastrous interview, example of, 122–130
Discourtesy, 95
Discussion sessions, with employees, 31, 32
Doorstep interview, 109–110
Down-the-line interview, 108–109
Dry run, of presentation, 29

Editorializing, 93, 117
Electronic equipment, tendency to go wrong, 29–30
Electronic mail, 18
Electronic media, 54
Empathy, 12, 13, 72, 93, 144–145
  lack of, 11
Employee:
  communications, 21–24
  disgruntled, 90
  forum, 30–32
  recalcitrant, to communicate with, 13
Entertainment, 93, 94, 112, 115, 117
Enthusiasm, 28, 139
Equipment failure, dealing with, 29–30
Executive-speak, 142–144
Experts, on television, 138–140, 142
Explanations, unsuitable for television, 78, 117
Eye contact, 28

Face-to-face press interview, 40–44
Failure, on television, 97, 115
Fear:
  of journalists, 88
  of public speaking, 24
Filtering process, 3
Flair, for speaking, 25–26
Flattery, 97–98
Floor manager, 100–101
Foolproof answers, 99, 116
Frame of reference, 11
Friction, within company, 81, 87

Gestures, 107
Grapevine, 22, 23
Green Room, 98–99

Hackneyed phrases, 20, 142–143
Hatchet job, example of, 132–133
Headgear, 106
Heath, Edward, 104
Home, Alec Douglas, 105
Homily, 74–75
Hospitality suite, 98
Hostility, of interviewer, 57, 114
Hosting a television crew, 131–137

'I', use of, 65–66
Iconoclasm, selective, 23
Imagery, 73–75
Impromptu interview, 109–110
Indifference, of television audience, 61
Influence, via the media, 13, 59, 102
Informality, of journalists, 38
Information:
  distillation, 77, 86
  inside, 90–91
  technology, useful to journalists, 90
Intentions, of sender, 14–15
Interrupting, 117–118
Interview format, 108–110
Interview model, 81–86
Interview programmes, 35
Interview, television, 77–78, 94–95, 97, 121
  disaster, example of, 122–130
  how to handle, 116–130

on home ground, 131–137
invitation to, 48, 92–93
how to look, 101–108
how not to sabotage, 97–101
training, early days, 54–59
Interviewer, television, 99–100, 114–118
Invitations, from media, 48, 92
Isolation, of television interview, 98, 100
Issues modelling, 82–87

Jargon, 71, 84–86, 141–143
Jewellery, 104–105
Journalism, 89
Journalists, 34, 38–40, 45, 87
characteristics, 88–89
job/role, 33, 44, 113, 133
local, 37
mission, 90–91
motivation, 89
trade/specialist, 37

Keyboard skills, 17–18
Knowledge, of viewing audience, 60–62

Language pitfalls, 65–67, 74
Letter, business, 19–21
Libel suits, 89
Live radio interview, preferable, 49–50
Local colour, 132
Local impact, of news, 37
Lying, detected by television, 79, 101

McLuhan, Marshall, 6
Major, John, 105, 119
Make-up, 101–102
Meaning, underlying, 4
Media proliferation, 79–80
Medium is the Message, The, 6
Memo, 15–19

Message, to convey, on television, 72–75
Messages:
analysing one's own, 9
how they are received, 1–2, 4
Metaphor, 75
Method acting, as way of achieving empathy, 12, 96
Mind pictures, *see* Imagery
Minder, for television crew, 135
Mishaps, in public speaking, 28–30
Multiple questions, 119–120

Name cards, 32
Naturalness, 139–140
Nervousness, 29
News coverage, 113
News planning meeting (television), 91, 93
Nixon, Richard, 101–102, 109
'No comment', reply to press, 39, 56
Non-attributable press briefing, 40
Number one shot, 61–62

Off-the-record press interview, 39–40
Office, as interview venue, 41–42, 132, 135–136
Office interview, 136–137
One-to-one interview (television), 108
'One', use of, 66–67
Opening techniques, in speech, 26
Orwell, George, 142–143
Overload, of communication, 2

Panel interview (television), 108
Photosensitive lenses, 105
Pictures, value of, in communication, 63–64, 73–74
Plausibility, on camera, 79
Point of view, 11
Powell, Enoch, 119
Practice interview, 99–100
Preparation, for television interview, 80–87

Presentations, 24-30
Presenter, *see* Interviewer, television
Press call, unexpected, 44-45
Press, condemnation of, 89
Press queries:
  face-to-face, 40-44
  handling questions, 38-39
  preparing for, 36-38
Press release, 32-36
Privacy, invasion of, 89, 91
Producer, 101
Production assistant, 97-98, 100
Prop, personal, 105
Public relations advice, use of, 92

Questioning a journalist, 38
Questions:
  following address, 25
  to deflect, 118-119
  hostile, 57, 114
  planted, 30-31

Radio broadcasting, 46-48
Radio interview, by telephone, 49-50
Radio session, in studio, 48-49
Rapport, with interviewer, 99-100
Reading, from script, 27
Receiver, of communication, 1-3
Reductive communication, 80, 86, 95
Refusing an interview, 92-93, 134
Rejection, of television camera, 110
Relaxed approach, 29, 31-32, 100
Reporter, *see* Journalists
Representative, of company, in television interview, 78-79, 121
Research, before television interview, 80-87
Researcher, television news, 92-93
Response, delayed:
  in dealing with mail, 18, 21
  in dealing with media, 134

Responsibility, of television appearance, 78-79
Restaurant, as venue for press interview, 42-44
Reticence, before television interview, 99, 100, 136-137
Rote memory, best avoided in public speaking, 27
Round-robin introduction session, 32
Royal family, and television, 112-113
Run-through, *see* Practice interview

Scene-setting, for effective communication, 13, 30-32
Scepticism, of employees, 22-23
Script, in public speaking, 27
Scrutiny, of self, 9-10
Second personal pronoun, 64-68
Security, at workplace, 133
Self-criticism, 9, 15
Self-deprecation, 97-98
Self-investigation, 9-10
Sender, intentions of, 14-15
Signals, in television studio, 101
Simile, 75
Simplification, of message, 67-69, 70, 71-72, 139-141, 143
Slack news period, to exploit, 34-35
Smoking, 107-108
Sources, of information, 90-91, 145
Spectacles, 105
Speech patterns, varied to suit situation, 9-10
Speed:
  of delivery, 28
  essential in employee communications, 22
Spontaneity:
  in press call, 44-45
  in public speaking, 27-28

INDEX

Stage management, of communication event, 13, 31-32
Stalling, 48, 92, 120
Statements, for television interview, 79-80, 86, 114
Story leads, 90-91
Storyline, 93, 117
Stringers, 90-91
Studio audience, 108
Studio, television, 62, 98, 100-101
Style, of press release, 33-34
Style, personal, 138-140
Style, written, 20-21, 23-24
Subject knowledge, 25
Sublanguage, 141-143
Subliminal message, 4, 106-107
Surface meaning, 4
Sweating, 101

Table, of psychological benefit, 31-32
Tabloid press, 37
Tactics, in press interview, 38-39
Tape recorder, at press interview, 42
Taped presentation, for commercial radio, 50-51
Taped radio interview, beware of editing, 49-50
Team involvement, to foster, 32
Telephone, as alternative to memo, 17
Telephone radio spot, 49-50
Television, 54, 112
  advertising revenue, 59, 111
  audience, 60-62, 63, 68
  a different medium, 55
  power of, 6, 59, 102, 138
  studio, 62, 98, 100-101
  training, 56-57

Television crews, 133-135
Television interview, *see* Interview, television
Televisual communication, effective, 64-76, 114-116, 121-122, 140, 145-146
Thatcher, Margaret, 103, 106-107, 118, 119
Time constraints, on television, 77-78, 117
Timing, of press release, 34-35
Truthfulness, in front of camera, 79

Unwillingness, to answer questions, 38-39

Venue, for press interview, 41-43
Viewer empathy, 65-66
Viewing public, 60-62, 68-72, 120
Vigilance, after television interview, 137
Visual aids, 26-27, 29
Voice, female, on television, 103

Walden, Brian, 94, 118
Wardrobe, for television appearance, 104-107
'We', use of, 66
Wilson, Harold, 118-119
Women, and television appearance, 102-103
Women, as peacemakers, 103
Working life, 22

'You', use of, 64-65